SURVIVING SIBLING LOSS:
The Invisible Thread that Connects Us Through Life and Death

DAWN DIRAIMONDO, PSY.D.

Surviving Sibling Loss: The Invisible Thread that Connects Us Through Life and Death
All Rights Reserved.
Copyright © 2021 Dawn DiRaimondo, Psy.D.
v3.0

The opinions expressed in this manuscript are solely the opinions of the author and do not represent the opinions or thoughts of the publisher. The author has represented and warranted full ownership and/or legal right to publish all the materials in this book.

This book may not be reproduced, transmitted, or stored in whole or in part by any means, including graphic, electronic, or mechanical without the express written consent of the publisher except in the case of brief quotations embodied in critical articles and reviews.

Outskirts Press, Inc.
http://www.outskirtspress.com

Paperback ISBN: 978-1-9772-3666-1
Hardback ISBN: 978-1-9772-2883-3

Library of Congress Control Number: 2020916571

Cover Photo © 2021 www.gettyimages.com. All rights reserved - used with permission.

Outskirts Press and the "OP" logo are trademarks belonging to Outskirts Press, Inc.

PRINTED IN THE UNITED STATES OF AMERICA

To my brother, Michael
And all of our deeply missed siblings

Table of Contents

Acknowledgments i
Introduction iii
Chapter 1: The Call 1
Chapter 2: The First Two Weeks 6
Chapter 3: The Twilight Zone: The Initial Shock. 10
Chapter 4: Stages of Grief and Wave Metaphor 14
Chapter 5: The New Version of Yourself,
    Your Family, and the New Normal 19
Chapter 6: The Dreaded Questions 26
Chapter 7: The Holidays, Birthdays & Anniversaries 29
Chapter 8: Making Time for Making Memories 33
Chapter 9: This Is Where things Get Weird:
    Signs, Mediums, and the Great Unknown 39
Chapter 10: The Chapter For Therapists and
    Ideas to Bring to Your Therapy 48
Chapter 11: The Interviews 55
Chapter 12: The Most Helpful Things We Did 76
Chapter 13: The Grieving Process in other Cultures
    and Religions 84
The Final Chapter: My Wish 91
Epilogue 94
Photo Gallery 95

Acknowledgments

Thank you to my parents, Tony and Carol, and sister, Dani, for your never ending love, support, and for allowing me to share our story. I treasure you.

Thank you to my husband, Josh, and children, Mikayla and Mason, for not only your love, support, and encouragement but also for understanding all the long days and late nights of writing as well as my preoccupation with this book over the last six months. And Mikayla for your help with the pictures and your amazing computer skills!

Thank you to my incredible extended family and the best cousins you could ask for. Special thank you to my cousin Chris, who has always treated me more like a sister and helped connect me to Trey. And thank you, Trey, for recommending Outskirts Press, the wonderful publishing company I partnered with to make this book a reality.

Thank you to the amazing community of friends in Simi Valley who supported my parents and our family all of these years. Your support and love were instrumental in our healing.

Thank you to all my dear friends who supported me when I lost Michael, as well as all of my friends and colleagues who encouraged me to write this book. Thank you to Danielle, Angie, Dani, Ted, and John, for your thoughtful feedback and helpful editing suggestions. So very grateful to you all.

And last but furthest from least, thank you to the sibling

bereavers who so graciously let me interview them: Annie, Angela, Dani, Jill, Jesse, Liz, Mark, Mary, Melissa, Michelle, Raychel, Rolanda, Samantha, Tomei and those names I am withholding for privacy purposes, you know who you are. I am deeply grateful you shared such personal stories about your siblings with me. These interviews were powerful, touching, and one of the most meaningful parts of this experience for me. Thank you for your honesty, vulnerability, and permission to share your stories and experiences so we can hopefully help others with their grief journeys. The deep love and connection felt for your siblings came through so powerfully in each and every interview. Thank you again, from the bottom of my heart.

Introduction

On January 8, 2004, I lost my brother, Michael. He was twenty-two years old and I was twenty-eight, a month shy of turning twenty-nine. Michael was deployed in Iraq, serving as a flight medic in the Army. I became a clinical psychologist five months before he died. I can't help but to write this book weaving both my personal experiences of losing my brother along with my professional knowledge of grief and loss and experiences with the clients in my private practice. My hope is that this combination of who I am adds value to this book. I have received permission to share any information involving my clients' stories and my fellow sibling bereavers who graciously allowed me to interview them and share their stories, for which I am deeply grateful.

This book will begin with my own story of being abruptly thrust into the world of grief and loss with the learning of the sudden death of my brother. I share my experiences of how this impacted me personally and professionally. I discuss common myths and beliefs about how grief works and the actual experience, told by myself and others who have also lost siblings. My goal is to help normalize reactions, symptoms, and experiences as well as provide hope and ideas on how to learn to live with the painful loss of a sibling. Ideas on ways to honor your sibling, as well as navigating through the holidays, birthdays, and other difficult days will also be shared.

They say significant loss is a club that nobody wants to

be a part of. This is true. However, if you are reading this, you are here, or you are somebody who wants to understand how to help and support someone who has recently experienced the loss of a sibling or loved one. This book is first and foremost for the siblings who are learning to live with the devastating loss of their sibling. However, I also hope this can be a useful guide to their family, friends, partners, and even therapists, to learn how to better understand and support them. With that said, I have included a chapter focused on ideas to bring to one's therapy, different types of therapies that may be useful to you, and information that may be helpful to therapists working with clients who are struggling with significant loss.

I also discuss how grief is not created equal and how deaths that are considered "biologically out of order," such as children and siblings dying before their parents and grandparents, are often felt the deepest and leave the biggest wounds and traumatic reactions, including nightmares, flashbacks, avoidance, numbness, severe depression, and anxiety, sometimes lasting years (especially if someone is not in professional treatment). As a result, these types of deaths need to be understood differently than, say, the loss of an elderly grandparent, and appropriate levels of support will often be required and recommended.

One of the many challenges of living with significant grief is the lacking vocabulary in American culture pertaining to bereavement. There simply aren't enough words to describe the feelings and experiences associated with grief, in part, I believe, because nobody wants to talk about it. This often feels extremely frustrating to people because it is hard to describe a feeling there isn't a word for in the English language. *Devastating* seems to be one of the strongest words we have to pull from, although "devastating" seems to better describe the effects of a destructive storm or an accident—all horrible without question. The death of a sibling or child is beyond devastating, but we don't have another word to name that feeling or experience. It is a level of brokenness that likely only another sibling or parent can truly understand. This limited language, therefore, makes even expressing grief with words that much more challenging.

I will also use the term *bereaver* and not *bereaved* because bereaved implies that the bereavement is in the past tense, and, as I will describe more in this book, sibling loss is a loss someone lives with throughout their entire lives. You don't "get over" or move on from significant loss; you change and you learn to live with the loss. That is not to say the bereavement is always the same; the process and experience certainly change over time, looking and feeling different throughout one's life. Bereavement lives inside us, as part of us, and for most of the outside world, they never even know. This invisible thread and connection to our lost sibling lives in our heart and changes who we are. So I use bereaver to reflect that this is a current, ongoing activity and more of a verb than something past tense.

One of my specialties in my private practice is to work with people who are experiencing significant loss, such as the loss of children, siblings, partners, and parents at a young age. I was inspired to finally write this book after learning from one of my clients—who had recently lost multiple siblings and family members within a short period of time—that there was still a sparse number of books written on and resources for sibling loss. This was also my experience in 2004 when I found little written about sibling loss. I was shocked and disappointed to learn that only a handful of books had been added to the literature since the time I lost my brother, sixteen years ago. Because there wasn't a lot written on sibling loss, I ended up reading books that covered grief in general and the loss of a child or spouse. However, these losses differ significantly, and I felt a deep need to write this book and have the sibling story be told as well. I want my experience to help others through some of the very darkest, most painful times of their lives. I also do this as yet another way to honor my brother's life and early death.

I will end this book with the ways I believe that this change is not all bad, despite how absolutely horrible it feels in the beginning, and may for a long time. In fact some of this change can help you live a more present, engaged, and purposeful life than those who do not experience significant loss until later in life. These changes can powerfully shift our priorities and bring us the very real awareness that, in fact, we all have a timeline; we just don't know what it is. And we stop taking time and relationships for granted.

I share some of the stories and messages shared with me during the interviews of fellow sibling bereavers as they recalled their memories and experiences with navigating through grief. I hope reading this book provides you some comfort in relating to some of these feelings, stories, and experiences; gives you some ideas that make sense to you in your journey through grief; and provides ways to process the loss of your sibling, ways to continue integrating them in your life and honoring them. Your sibling(s) are a powerful part of your story, who you are, where you came from, and how you have or will change as a result of losing them. The invisible thread, well intact even through death, keeps us connected. Hold them in your heart; they get to be yours forever there.

Chapter 1

THE CALL

Thursday January 8, 2004

The morning began quite ordinary, by all accounts, leaving me completely unprepared for the call that would soon unravel my world. I remember looking over at the black phone ringing in my small office. I had a feeling that I didn't want to answer it and was supposed to be leaving for a meeting shortly. I had recently been licensed as a clinical psychologist and this was my first job at an agency that served families and children in Sacramento.

I noticed a news report online earlier that a Blackhawk helicopter had been shot down in Fallujah, Iraq, where my brother, Michael had been serving in the Army as a flight medic for nearly a year. I tried not to worry when I heard reports like this; he was always fine and it didn't help to worry. We wrote letters back and forth, and we last talked to him on Christmas Day. It was a mere six more weeks until he was scheduled to come home. Michael was the youngest of three children at twenty-two. I was the oldest at a month shy of twenty-nine, and my sister, Dani, was in the middle at twenty-six years old.

The phone rang again. *I better answer this*, I thought. My sister was on the other end.

Her voice was shaken and upset, almost desperate and surprised-sounding. "You haven't talked to Dad yet?"

"No, why?" I asked.

"You haven't talked to Dad yet?!" she asked, this time even more upset and surprised. I later learned that Dani had known for the last hour that Michael died, but my father had been unable to reach me. Dani realized in this moment that I didn't know yet, and she had to tell me.

"No…" My voice more apprehensive now.

"Michael was killed!"

I didn't say anything. It was as if time stood still. I just froze.

"Did you hear me?!" she asked.

"Yes" was all I could say.

Now growing more confused and frustrated with my seeming lack of response, she added firmly, "You need to come home!"

"Okay" I responded.

"You need to come home now!" This time more forceful.

"Okay, I will."

"Nothing will ever be the same again!" I remember her saying as she cried.

"Okay, I'll come home," I told her again. I was often the peacemaker in my family, the family therapist at times, if you will. But this, this I couldn't really process. And there was nothing reassuring I could think of to say back to her.

When I went to tell my supervisor, I could see the look of shock, horror, and sadness in her eyes. I remember saying, "In case I'm not back by Monday..." This was on a Thursday. She stopped me and said, "Dawn. You won't be back on Monday. You will probably be out for a couple of weeks."

A couple of weeks? Right, probably. She asked how she could help and I remember asking for her to change my voicemail. I couldn't do it. She agreed and asked if there was anything I needed, to let her know.

As a therapist working with people with significant anxiety, depression, attachment, and abandonment issues, leaving for two weeks without any notice or warning was difficult for me. I could hardly process it all.

I just leave? I thought. Maybe my strong work ethic and frozen response were at play because I seemed confused. I just go home right now? I must have shared this concern with the psychologist whose office was right next to mine, and I still remember her clearly and compassionately telling me that the needs there would always be there; where I needed to be was with my family right now. I still remember that and how it helped give me permission to let the work part of me go and be with my family.

Even when I came back, some clients asked why I was away. I said it was a family emergency and that I was sorry but I couldn't talk about it further. And I truly couldn't; it was too raw, too real, and too vulnerable. They shared their biggest hurts, but I couldn't share mine. Not yet anyway. That time would come.

Somehow, I drove myself home. I remember thinking I was surprised I could drive at all and was shaking but knew I just needed to keep driving and get home.

My father had tried calling me several times that day but hadn't been able to reach me. I called back when I got home and all I can remember was my mom crying and him saying to me, "It's true! It's true! He's gone!" He handed someone else the phone and I could hear him crying hysterically in the background. As if having to tell me and say it out loud again made it even more real and added another puncture in his heart. I'm not sure if I had seen my father cry before then, maybe once, but I can assure you, I had never heard him cry like that before. It was as deep a cry as you could hear. My mom was screaming. Shit just got real. I was still in a mostly frozen, shaken state, but the effects of the bomb that went off in my family were starting to seep in.

I don't even remember telling my then boyfriend, now husband. He and a friend picked me up and drove me to the airport. Within three hours of the call, I was on a plane for Sacramento and flying to Simi Valley, where my parents lived. Just like that, in one moment, one call, my life and family changed forever. And in three hours flat, I left everything and would never return the same again.

*Healing Hands,
a Compassionate Heart
and a Smile that Lights Up Heaven*

~ On Michael's headstone,
written by my father,
Tony DiRaimondo

Chapter 2

The First Two Weeks

People came from everywhere. Our family and friends from New York, New Jersey, Texas, Boston, Las Vegas, even as far away as Prague. Friends from Sacramento, all over Southern California, my brother's friends, and our family friends from Simi Valley and probably many other places I am unaware of. All of our family and friends, everyone showed up, came to the house, came to the wake, the services. The house was filled with people. My cousin Matthew even mailed bagels from New York. This might seem odd, but my parents were born and raised in Brooklyn, New York, and despite many things we don't remember from this time, they sure remember that sweet gesture.

Michael was a good-looking kid with a big, bright smile

and a sweet, funny, and compassionate personality. He had a good sense of humor, lots of friends, and many people who loved him. He was the youngest of ten cousins on my mother's side. This wasn't just our loss; they all loved Michael. Our family, his friends, and the huge community of family friends were with us, and their support then and through the years has been amazing. I am forever grateful. We would have absolutely not gotten through this the way we have without everyone's support.

I can see why people bring food to those who recently lost someone, because it actually helps. You don't have the energy or interest in preparing food, and if it wasn't sitting in front of you, it would be very easy not to eat. Plus, people want some way to help. And the flowers help too. You wouldn't think they would, but flower arrangements were everywhere and although I can't remember any of them specifically, I can tell you that it mattered that they were there. All the people showing up matters. It makes you feel that your pain matters, their life and your loss *matters,* and I will never forget how much love I felt from it all.

Those first two weeks were filled with lots of people around us. Lots of crying and even lots of singing. One of my sister's friends, Cole, must have mentioned playing the guitar, so he brought that over and he and my father sang and played the guitar. We all slowly joined in to "Take Me Home Country Roads" and "Back Home Again" by John Denver, songs we grew up to my dad singing to us. Our living room was filled with people singing. And just to be clear, we don't do this with people; actually my dad hadn't pulled his guitar out in years. But it felt like we were singing to Michael, giving him permission somehow to go where he needed to go. That we would always be connected to him, we would figure out a way to be okay, and we would always love him. Maybe we welcomed his spirit home. It felt healing and beautiful.

And in this grieving and love and connection, creativity emerged. Cole ended up writing and recording a beautiful song for us about my brother and our experience of losing him, which we called "Michael's Song." My cousin Vinny (yes, we are one big Italian family) thought of the idea to make shirts to memorialize my brother. The Los Angeles-based advertising agency my sister worked at paid for them to be made. They had a picture of Michael sitting in his helicopter with the words: Gone but Not Forgotten. We all wore the shirts and gave them out at the wake.

We also decided we wanted a slide show of pictures to music for the wake (Catholics do this the night before the funeral) and CDs of music that reminded us of Michael to give out to everyone as well. My parents, my sister, Michael's friends, and I all contributed song ideas that represented Michael. My sister and I picked "Love Me When I'm Gone" by Three Doors Down, and my father wanted "Proud to Be an American" by Lee Greenwood. Our family friend, Ryan, made hundreds of copies of the CDs for us. We gave them to everyone. When I wanted to connect with Michael, I would play the CD and even now feel like it is his way of saying hello when a song comes on the radio or Pandora.

Although you would never imagine you would want to take pictures or videos of services, I would actually recommend it. And if anyone speaks at a service or memorial, ask them to give you a copy of what they said. I remember very little and it is really nice to save and re-read later. Some people did this for us, which I am grateful for.

The funeral at St. Peter Claver Church in Simi Valley was standing-room only. There must have been a thousand people there. Simi Valley is a very patriotic town and at this point in the Iraq war in 2004, Michael was the first service member who had died from Simi Valley in military action since the Vietnam War. The church was packed and the city gave us a police and fire department escort from the church to the cemetery. It was totally unbelievable. I just wish I could have seen my brother's reaction. I think he would have been as equally in awe. It was like he was the president or something. The media called the house a lot, and my parents spoke with all of them. They were in the newspapers and on the local news. It was all so incredibly surreal. I will forever be grateful to our community, friends, cousins, and extended family for all of their love and support in helping us cope and heal through losing my brother.

However, despite all of this love and support around us, I still woke up every single morning to the sounds of my mother screaming and crying. "No! No! I want him back! I want him back!" This would go on for what felt like hours. My cousin Darren is a physician and ended up recommending she be prescribed a small amount of Xanax to help her through the worst of these episodes and to help her fall asleep at night. Although this initially took some convincing, sometimes it seemed like the only thing that helped her calm down. Even recalling this as I write it down is painful. The pain was piercing. And although I felt bad leaving my parents after two weeks, it was also too hard to stay any longer.

Chapter 3

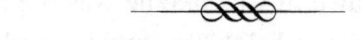

THE TWILIGHT ZONE: THE INITIAL SHOCK.

You don't know what day it is, if you have eaten yet or what you ate; you can't concentrate, your memory is shot, and often you feel physical pain in your heart and a pervasive feeling of exhaustion. And yet the world around you carries on as if nothing happened, like they don't know, like it doesn't matter. The outside looks like it always has, but on the inside, you feel like the world has been turned upside down and inside out, and you have no idea how you will survive this or who you will be when the dust settles.

We learned that Michael's helicopter had been shot down and all nine individuals on board, crew members and patients, were killed. A second Army Blackhawk helicopter was there and tried reviving them, but nobody could be saved. We spoke with Michael's friend who was on that second helicopter and we found comfort that he was there with Michael, held him, devastated his efforts couldn't save him. Despite landing hard, the helicopter didn't explode, and we therefore were given the option to have an open casket at his funeral. I am grateful for that option- but this was not an option any of us wanted. Seeing Michael like that would have been too hard for all of us. All four of us, my parents, sister, and I, were very clear that we couldn't see him lying in a casket. So still and so not alive. Maybe it would have provided some "closure," but closure isn't what we wanted.

In my practice, I have also had clients talk about loss feeling "less real" when they don't see their loved ones' bodies and "more real" when they have. Truthfully, maybe a small part of me and maybe even the rest of my family wanted to maintain this minute possibility that it wasn't real. Maybe they made a mistake or he was really a part of some secret mission and would reappear someday. Just a small part of me wanted to believe this could be true, and seeing him would have taken that away.

Michael had worked so hard to join the 571st Medical Company (Air Ambulance). Originally his company first sergeant said Michael was "too young, too green, and too under-ranked" to join this elite unit, but they gave him a chance and put him through the toughest ninety-day training and testing program they could set up. Michael completed this in forty-five days, the fastest that any soldier of any age, any rank, and any skill level had ever completed the course at the 571st Medical Company. During his deployment in Iraq, Michael went on to earn a Bronze Star, an Air Medal, an Air Medal with Valor for his skills and bravery in a hostile situation, and the Purple Heart.

Michael was so proud and loved his work as a flight medic. He loved helping people and finally found his passion and calling. Sometimes people would ask if I was angry about the war or if I would ever let my own children join the military. I didn't put my energy toward anger or the war. I had to focus on healing and grieving. And I firmly believe that finding your passion in life is one of the most important, most soulful experiences of our lives. If finding his passion led Michael to lose his life, it was still a mission he had to take. Some people never find their passion. I know this because I hear the pain it causes in my clients, wondering if there was more they should do, wondering what else they may have been meant for, and this can almost be haunting to them: feeling left out of a purpose or calling they see others experiencing and the meaning that brings to their lives.

Instead, we would carry the haunting. The deep sadness in missing, the sadness in feeling robbed of so much. His life cut so short, so few years. And truthfully, my biggest fear with him away at war was of him getting kidnapped and not knowing what was happening to him. My spiritual beliefs are unwavering that he is in a place of peace and love. I call that place heaven but not because I identify with any particular religion. I believe in a higher power, a God, but I don't need others to agree with this same belief or even use the same words. I believe Michael lives in another dimension and in that place nobody can hurt him. So we suffer instead,

I suffer, my family suffers, but he didn't. We were told by the military and several mediums—I will get into more detail later in the book—that he died instantly. "I was here, and then I was there. Just like that." No pain. No goodbyes.

Chapter 4

STAGES OF GRIEF AND WAVE METAPHOR

You begin to deeply miss physically seeing your sibling. It's as if your brain scans the crowds looking for them. I would borrow strangers who resembled my brother and stare at them, trying to be discreet of course, but soaking in what my eyes and heart missed so much—his face, his smile.

Sibling loss is felt to the core. Not only do you lose someone, but possibly the only person who has a shared childhood with you, knows your family the way you do, and is a part of you—but you also lose a part of yourself and your world. And although the effects may shift and change over time, they last your entire life.

Attachment is a feeling, an internal experience. We get attached to people, pets, places, things, and even ideas. Our attachments end up shaping our lives, and this invisible thread links us to others, superseding distance, time, and most certainly death. I wish we could see these threads, but instead we are left to just feel them. And these attachments end up being some of, if not *the most,* important, meaningful parts of our lives.

It is said that our grief reflects our love. This love and therefore grief can be quite intense. Your heart and soul aren't the only things aching; your brain isn't working the same either. Your ability to concentrate, focus, process information and your memory are all impacted initially and possibly for months, maybe longer.

"Normal" grief symptoms, according to the *Diagnostic and Statistical Manual of Mental Disorders, Fifth edition,* known as the DSM-V, states that typical grief symptoms can include difficulty concentrating, fatigue, impaired memory, loss of appetite, depression, anxiety, startle response, difficulty sleeping, or increased sleeping, in some cases, even dreams, hallucinations, or visions of a loved one who has died. Experiences such as physical pain and avoidance also can occur. These experiences can last for days, weeks, months, even years. If symptoms last more than a few weeks or are so severe that they interfere with someone's ability to take care of themselves or work, they likely need professional support.

One of the most misunderstood theories on grief is the five stages of grief developed by Dr. Elisabeth Kübler-Ross, a psychiatrist and pioneer in grief work. She was the author of *On Death and Dying* amongst others. The five stages in the Kübler-Ross model are Denial, Anger, Bargaining, Depression, and Acceptance. However, Dr. Kübler-Ross never intended or suggested that these stages and/or feelings be experienced as linear. They are not linear; they can happen out of order and even simultaneously. They are some of the experiences and feelings people have when they are dying or losing someone. It doesn't surprise me that American culture, which loves "five easy steps" to everything, would initially see this as something you start and finish in order and then successfully complete. The hope being that someone would essentially then be finished with the grieving process, feel much less emotionally impacted by their loss, and be ready to move on with their life. Unfortunately, the experience and emotions of grief don't function like that; it is a much more fluid and complex process. However, the wave analogy, now that one is spot-on.

The rhythm of grief is much more like waves. You can feel like you are completely knocked over by a huge wave, left devastated and broken, gasping for air. Then the wave recedes and there is a calm, until the next set rolls in and more waves hit you. At first it can feel like this happens over and over; waves of emotion and memories coming frequently, leaving you in a puddle of tears or fits of anger, intensely in touch with your grief and pain. But over time the waves diminish in size and intensity, and you have more time in between them. Sometimes people can be discouraged by the waves' return, feeling like they had been "doing so much better" or "hadn't cried in days or weeks." I remind my clients that the rogue waves can come out of nowhere and knock you over when you least expect it. All part of the grieving process. Sometimes you will be triggered by a song, something you saw, remembered, even smelled, someone's cologne or perfume. Sometimes, however, the waves seem to come out of nowhere. But again, over time, the waves are fewer and breaks in between, longer.

When does this get easier? It does get easier. I think it's important to know that it won't always be so raw; it won't always hurt so much. The physical pain and shock diminish over time. You learn to live with the missing. I asked a number of parents who lost children when there was a sense of normalcy again, and "five years" most often came up. Although I know from my own experience and with clients, some feel guilty over feeling better. They never want this to feel okay. My own mother worried if people saw her laugh they would judge her for being able to be happy or smile despite losing her son. It is hard to put a time frame on when *better* occurs, but I know that I wanted to know and I assume others reading this might be wondering as well. I suppose the first couple of years are the worst, but it feels like the real answer is that you change, and time is experienced and felt so differently with grief.

As mentioned earlier in the chapter, the physical and emotional effects of grief are very real and can make working and your daily routine feel quite challenging. Modifying your schedule, such as working part time if possible, will likely be helpful, at least in the beginning. However, too much unstructured alone time is not your friend either. Grief is intense, painful, and exhausting. You need breaks from it too. Some distraction can actually serve you, give you some much-needed reprieve. Be careful not to distract, avoid, or stay so busy you don't leave any time for your grief. These feelings are important to feel, albeit difficult.

For some, though, the grief feels so unbearable and overwhelming, they turn to other means of escape: drinking, drugs, gambling, anything to feel less or not feel at all. Others try denying or minimizing their feelings and notice that they develop psychosomatic symptoms, such as stomachaches, headaches, and chronic pain. As trauma therapist Dr. Bessel Van der Kolk wrote in his book *The Body Keeps the Score,* our body holds on to memories and feelings as well, especially if we don't (or can't) acknowledge them.

These feelings need to be known, heard, and processed or they will live in your body. There is no shortcut or way to speed up the process. Grief will wait—maybe until you are sleeping, and then come through in a dream or nightmare, or surface when you are intoxicated and your defenses are down. Grief is expressed through your body and can be experienced through pain and discomfort. But your psyche will wait until you address the loss, acknowledge and work through the feelings until they truly become less raw and haunting, and move toward a quieter space, where the love, peace, and memories live.

Chapter 5

The New Version of Yourself, Your Family, and the New Normal

The best way to describe how I felt when I lost my brother was that part of me died too. It felt like part of me went with him, wherever he is now, and part of him stayed with me and all the people who also loved and felt connected to him. I believe this is one of the reasons why we sometimes can feel more connected to our siblings when we are in the presence of others who also carry a part of our siblings in them. There were over six years between me and Michael, and I always felt very maternal toward him. Even when he was a baby, I enjoyed playing with him and taking care of him.

I felt like I had broken into a million pieces after he died and then slowly got put back together over time, but not the same as before. Friends looked at me like I was the same person, which helped me feel like there was still a cohesive *me* to be found, but nothing felt cohesive on the inside. And looking into the eyes of my devastated parents and sister reminded me how far from okay we were and the long road to recovery ahead of us.

Everyone grieves differently. So my father and I were more private with our sadness, whereas my sister and mother cried more in front of others; their tears came more easily. Irritability is what came up more easily for me and with a vengeance. I felt more jaded…so much less patient. Gone was the sweet person I remember being and in her place, this new version I barely recognized. I remember the fatigue as well; grief is exhausting. And there is little energy left for niceties or bullshit—there just isn't. You are literally in survival mode, just getting through each day. I remember crying in the shower or in my car. I didn't cry with other people. It wasn't that I didn't want to, I just couldn't.

On the outside I might not have looked like I needed support, but on the inside I did. I even asked my husband, Josh, to ask me how I was doing and told him that when I said fine, to ask me how I was *really* doing. I needed both of us to take an extra step to get to my feelings about my brother. I needed him to ask and know how I felt. I needed it to be on his radar too. Because I lost my brother in my late twenties, most people my age couldn't relate to losing a sibling or significant loss. With the exception of my sister, I didn't know anyone who had also lost their sibling. My friends and husband didn't understand this new place I lived in, feeling half dead, disoriented, and *so* tired. They loved me but they couldn't really understand what I was going through.

My clients who lose significant family members such as parents at a young age or siblings as a young person have also found that their same-age peers have little experience with this level of loss. As a result, many people talk about feeling very alone with their grief. I have even suggested to my clients that they ask their friends or partners, if they have one, to check in with them, to ask how they are feeling about their loss. It is not uncommon for people in their twenties to not experience significant loss for many years, if not decades, so it leaves the younger bereaved person feeling very alone.

My sister even specifically asked her best friend to make a note in her calendar every January 8th, the anniversary of Michael's passing, to remember to ask her how she was doing. Dani needed at least one person outside of our family to know what this date meant for her. This was back before social media became what it is today. I will discuss this later in the book, but I do think one of the benefits of social media is that it is a platform to share information like this—pictures, posts, memorials—and it allows others to support and engage with you on the important dates such as our loved ones' birthdays and the anniversary of their passing. I have definitely felt a lot of support and love from these posts and people's comments. I enjoy hearing from my brother's friends over the years and love knowing that so many people still love, miss, and remember him. That really helps. One of people's biggest fears is that their siblings and loved ones will be forgotten over time.

The other very unexpected issue that comes up is how your friends react. The people you assumed would be the most supportive aren't always, and people you weren't as close to before surprisingly are. Then there are those people you never saw coming, who didn't even know you or your sibling before they died. Enter Mark Shuster and his family. Mark was a member of the local Marine Corps League and since Michael was killed in action, local Marines and Sailors wanted to show their support. Mark called our house and offered condolences to my parents on their behalf. He attended the church services, along with several other Marines, Sailors and service members from all military branches of service, both Active Duty and Veterans. Mark went on to become a very close friend to our family and an integral part of our support system.

Sometimes losing a sibling creates what I would call a birth order change or restructure that changes your experience in your family. Maybe losing your brother or sister leaves you an only child, leaves you now the youngest, oldest, or only girl, only boy, all of which changes you and your family. Losing my brother also meant our family surname, DiRaimondo, would not be passed on to future generations, another sad reality for us and especially for my Sicilian father. You feel robbed of a present, and robbed of a future as well. You can't help but feel robbed of not just time with them, but also the future children, nieces, nephews, and cousins. So much feels taken at once, never to be lived into, never to be realized.

I watched my parents change a lot too. I was raised with

beliefs such as "good things happen to good people." My parents used to have signs up before losing Michael that said, "This too shall pass"; well, that was all taken down with swiftness. My father didn't even believe in God or an afterlife before this, although he certainly does now. My belief system is so clear now that there is an afterlife (although I certainly am not clear on what all that entails), but I don't need others to agree or believe what I do. We grew much more spiritual as a family. We not only grieved my brother but also found ways to stay connected to him and keep him integrated into our family.

Double trauma

To see your parents heartbroken and shattered is beyond painful. The double blow or double trauma of sibling loss is that you don't just lose your sibling. You lose your parents for a while too, and your family as you had always known it. This isn't to say my parents weren't there for us, but the loss of a child is very different from the loss of a sibling. The pain was on their faces, in their voices; the pain filled the house and was present in most conversations for a long, long time.

The other issue that comes up in families is the issue of people grieving differently. For my mother, she needed and wanted to talk about her pain and grief often. Luckily, she received enormous support from her friends and family. Others are more private about their grief and don't want to talk about this with others.

My sister, father, and I were more private. We certainly wanted to talk about my brother with others but didn't seek out or ask for support as much from people. And truthfully, there were even times we needed breaks from talking about losing Michael with our parents. Dani and I were in our twenties; dating, building our careers and lives. We didn't always want to focus or reflect on the sadness and missing as much as they needed or wanted to. It became a balancing act of giving my parents the support they needed with the space and breaks that we sometimes needed. I know from the interviews I did for this book with other sibling bereavers that this was a common experience, feeling pulled between wanting to be there for your parents and struggling to manage your own loss, all while feeling lost in the process with most support going to your parents.

The New Normal

For myself, it feels very clear there is no moving on. That leaves out all of the significant change and impact that happens. You do eventually adjust to the New Normal and learn to live with grief, the missing, and the loss. Although the first year was by far the hardest, the second was tough too, the missing so hard and present. It took several years for the dust to start settling from the bomb that went off in my family and for this new way of being and living. However, life continued, love continued, and in the summer of 2007, a baby girl came into our lives.

My daughter Mikayla was born, named after her Uncle Michael. She was not only my firstborn but the first grandchild and first niece. My mom would hold her and kiss her as a baby, and Mikayla helped heal her heart. She helped heal us all. Mikayla didn't replace Michael, but she was a new being to love and hold and cuddle, and my mom would repeatedly say to me, "I love her SO much. Thank you so much for having her." It made my heart smile when she would say that. It was nice to see my mom smile and have moments of joy and happiness again. Although like any good experience, there was always a bittersweet feeling that Michael wasn't a part of these moments. He would never meet Mikayla, or my son, Mason, or my sister's children, Ellie and Natalie. For that matter, he never even met my husband, Josh, or brothers-in-law, John or Norman. However, they all know of Michael, and for the kids, their Uncle Michael is a powerful part of our family story and always will be.

Chapter 6

THE DREADED QUESTIONS

    It's a question that just comes up. You can even feel it coming before people so innocently ask, "So…how many siblings do you have?" And the dreaded question for parents: "How many children do you have?" In your heart, the answer is very clear. The number you always had. I have one sister and one brother; I am the oldest of three. And then what question often comes next? Any parent who has lost a child knows where this is going… "Oh, and how old are they?" Crap. Well, now here's the conundrum. Do you tell this person you don't even know who is probably just trying to be polite and curious by nature that you in fact lost a sibling and/or child and start crying or have your eyes fill up with tears and your voice crack? Because that isn't super awkward for all parties involved. Or do you say what their ages would have been now? That seems wrong too.

The dilemma is that it feels like you are betraying your sibling and/or child to leave them out. And that feels deeply wrong. I think this question gets easier with time. Sometimes I can tolerate just saying "I have a sister," depending on the circumstances, and other times I say that I have a sister and brother. If they ask about ages, I tell them my sister's age and that I lost my brother when he was twenty-two. Most people wish they had never asked at that point and typically are more than happy to move on to your questions: "How many siblings and/or children do you have?" "Are you originally from this area?" Anything will do... If they are a fellow bereaver of significant loss, sometimes they share their own story. This is by far less often but the conversation shifts to the known place of pain. This person has been through this experience and is living with it too. The curious person in me will sometimes even respond, "Oh no, can I ask how you lost them?" Depending on how long ago it was or under what condition, that might be one of their dreaded questions, but for others, it is an opportunity to talk about their loved one. I know when someone tells me first, I will also share my loss. It feels like a way of saying, "I too know significant loss and pain. I too am a member of the club that nobody wants to be a part of."

The next dreaded question is likely one most people who haven't been through this would never think of. You are walking into a restaurant with your family and the first question you are asked is "How many people in your party?" Crushing. For us we were a party of five. Always. I would rather invite someone to join or not go out—anything to avoid having to say, or hear my father say, "Four." Again, this is another question that hurts less over time. In part, because now my sister and I have families of our own and there are very few occasions where we would go out, just the four of us. However, I hated that question for years.

Chapter 7

The Holidays, Birthdays & Anniversaries

Since we lost Michael on January 8th of 2004, we had almost a year before we had to endure the first holiday season without him. I suppose that helped some, but there is no escaping that the firsts of holidays, birthdays, and the anniversary of a loved one's passing are filled with dread, anticipation, anxiety, deep missing, and a whole range of feelings: sadness, anger, maybe even jealousy. The holidays are of course especially hard because there is no getting away from them. Society is dripping in everything Christmas for months before it happens, and you can't go almost anywhere without a reminder. Decorations, music, pumpkin spice everything, everywhere.

The first Christmas my parents didn't even want to be home. We went to a hotel in Huntington Beach for a change of environment and our best effort to get away from Christmas. Given that my father was in the hotel business, staying in a hotel was like home away from home for us. We also didn't want to be with extended family yet since they still celebrated Christmas and rightfully so. We didn't want it to be just the four of us. It was way too sad and my brother's presence so painfully missed. We asked family friends, Steve and Rali, a young couple who didn't have children yet, if they would join us. They loved Michael too and didn't mind or feel uncomfortable with us talking about him and expressing sadness. They also brought a bit of laughter and love to help the dynamic feel more tolerable. I will forever be grateful to Steve and Rali for helping us through that first Christmas.

In my practice, I also see the parents who have lost children wish they could skip the holidays or do something completely different. This is particularly difficult if people still have other children, especially young children. Children don't share the same need to skip the holidays or want Santa to skip their house. They actually have a deep need for some sense of normalcy and still want some of the traditions to continue, and it is important for them to have some of these experiences. A family needs to discuss and come up with a plan that works for everyone, although compromise will likely be a part of this.

My mother was Ms. Christmas before we lost Michael. After that, Christmas came to a screeching halt. I don't think she decorated her house for nearly five years. And the only reason she did that again was for my daughter, Mikayla. She wanted to bring back the lights and decorations for her to see and enjoy. Mikayla was born three and a half years after Michael died. Although it took several years before stockings went back up, they did eventually. Because the look and feel of an empty stocking didn't sit well with us, we made a tradition of writing notes to fill Michael's stocking. We wrote down our favorite memories of him. Or we wrote letters to him. It felt like a way to include and integrate him into the holidays with us.

We also did things like adopting a family for Christmas. We wanted to do something to honor Michael. It felt better to give to those in need, and we would go shopping for kids with the clothes size given and wish lists.

On Michael's birthday, June 2nd, I would call my parents and we would sing to him. I would buy birthday cards for him and mail them to my parents' home. The wording would be tricky. The cards would read something like, "Although we don't see each other much these days, you are always in my heart" or things like that. We weren't in denial he wasn't with us, but honoring his birth felt right. Just because someone isn't physically with us or alive doesn't mean they never existed. We would also make donations to his foundation on his birthday. I usually made a donation for $45, since that was a number that reminded us of him. Forty-five had been his pager number in high school in the late nineties (before cell phones were what they are now, if you can even imagine that). I know some of Michael's friends went on a camping trip every year around Mike's birthday also to remember and honor him.

We ended up thinking of January 8th, the day Michael

passed away, as his birthday in heaven. Although we were all raised Catholic, we identify as much more spiritual than religious. We don't attend church regularly, but we have a strong faith and belief system in an afterlife where we believe Michael is and where we will be with him again someday. We believe he is alive and well there and we want to honor the beginning of his time there versus just the end of his time here.

Chapter 8

MAKING TIME FOR MAKING MEMORIES

Michael and I were six years apart. He was twelve years old when I went away to college, so I feel like I missed a lot of his teen years. He came to visit me in both Santa Cruz when I was in college and then San Francisco, during my years in graduate school—visits and memories I treasure. One of my favorite memories is the time I secretly took him skydiving when he turned eighteen. I knew my mom would worry, so we didn't call her until we hit the ground and were back in the car. Then we called her and said, "Guess what we just did?! We jumped out of a plane at ten thousand feet!" Of course she said, "You did what?! You are supposed to be a good influence on him!" Of course she was just glad we called her when we were safely on the ground and it was over. Truthfully though, when I first did this at twenty years old, it literally never occurred to me that maybe the shoot wouldn't open. However, by twenty-four, with my eighteen-year-old brother jumping after me, I nearly hyperventilated the whole way down, praying both of our shoots would open and we would land safely. He had a blast though and it was awesome to do together. I'm truly grateful for that memory.

One of my favorite quotes that I have seen posted on Facebook is the one that says, "Take vacations. Go as many places as you can. You can always make money. You can't always make memories," Unfortunately, I could not find the author of this wise statement. I live by this now. I am so glad I had my brother come visit me in college and graduate school, and we went to see him in Colorado before he left for Iraq. These are precious memories I wouldn't have if I didn't prioritize them or was "just too busy." And the truth is, life *is* very busy. As a mother now of a twelve and nine-year-old and a busy practice, life is very full. But one of my favorite ways to spend time and connect with my family is by going on vacations and having adventures with them. And my husband and I make this a priority.

You don't take the house, car, and all your stuff with you. I do believe though you take your memories, experiences, and love with you (didn't we learn that from Patrick Swayze in *Ghost*??). But in all seriousness, would you make different choices if you knew that you took your memories and relationships with you into death? Does your calendar match what you're saying your priorities are? Losing someone we love deeply has a powerful way of helping us reevaluate our choices, our jobs, and who we are spending time with.

In fact, at the time I lost my brother, I was working for an agency that kept moving in a direction I didn't sign up for when I was first hired. There was constant pressure on having enough "billable hours." They wanted us to start doing in-home therapy, something I wasn't comfortable with or willing to do. I was offered the opportunity to work in a private practice setting with an established psychiatrist, and despite the anxiety and uncertainties that go along with taking such a leap into self-employment, my grief was so much bigger that the anxiety took a backseat. I also knew life was too short to compromise and be unhappy. I certainly didn't go through all that schooling and student loan debt to be settling and unfulfilled. That was one of the best decisions of my life and I have never looked back. My private practice and the clients I have worked with over the years have been one of the biggest joys of my life. Our work feels sacred to me and I feel truly blessed to know them and that they allow me to be a part of their journeys.

I am in a unique position in my practice where I get a close look at when things go well in families and when things don't go well. I have tried borrowing these lessons in my own parenting. I see when family systems and dynamics create environments that leave teens and young adults feeling empty, lonely, and depressed. These are often families where there is a lot of detachment, people are in their separate rooms often, and nobody really knows how anybody else feels. When conflicts occur, they aren't worked through or discussed again. Avoidance and discord are more common. Sometimes these parents are struggling with their own depression, anxiety, and trauma histories but have never had their own treatment or help. One of the greatest gifts we can give our children and ourselves is to do our own work, "make sense of our lives" as Daniel Siegel, MD, psychiatrist and author of *Parenting From the Inside Out*, says. We need to know our triggers, issues, and unresolved hurts so we can live a life with awareness and intention and not unconsciously impact our children.

In the families of young adults with the strongest, most secure sense of self, their family stories have detailed, fun memories of together time as a family, family vacations, dinners together. These don't need to be expensive trips per se; rather the key is that they do things together in a memorable way, they celebrate each other, and they *know* each other. The parents are curious and attuned with their kids' feelings and needs. These kids feel loved, cared about, and an important part of their families. When conflict or disruptions happen in these families, attempts at repair are made. Discussions are had and agreements and efforts to do things differently in the future are made.

If you are reading this and want to change your family dynamic, I truly believe repair and healing can happen at any age. Even if you have big kids now in their forties or fifties, anybody wants to hear a well-deserved apology or know what they mean to you. I know someone who was in his seventies and was at his ninety-five-year-old father's deathbed. When his father whispered for him to come closer, he really thought he might be finally getting a long overdue apology for the hurtful, abusive upbringing he endured as a child and young man. Unfortunately, his father was just asking for water and never got the apology he longed for and deserved from his poor childhood treatment. Point being, apologies matter, at any age. Repair what needs to be repaired. I have had more than one client tell me that they never once heard their mother say she was sorry. One of my lessons that I have taken from my clients: I definitely model apologies for my kids now. We do what we are shown.

Why address family dynamics in this book? Because losing a sibling or significant loved one has a way of rocking you to your core and creates an opportunity to reevaluate how things are going in your life, your job, and your relationships. Significant shifts often happen in this reflective space, and what really matters to you becomes clearer. What matters less, often gets left behind as it doesn't fit into this new chapter of your life.

So if you want to raise your family differently than you were, do it. But you have to make a very conscious decision how you will do things differently; if not we all operate from our unconscious defaults of how we were raised. Do the work on yourself. There are many paths to this; maybe that means therapy, meditation, yoga, or all of the above. And you will not only change yourself but your relationships as well, for generations to come. Oh, and book that vacation too.

And if I go, while you're still here…
Know that I live on,
Vibrating to a different measure
behind a thin veil you cannot see through.

You will not see me,
So you must have faith.
I wait for the time when we can soar
 together again,
both aware of each other.

Until then, live your life to its fullest.
And when you need me, just whisper
 my name in your heart,
…I will be there.

-Colleen Corah Hitchcock

Chapter 9

This Is Where things Get Weird: Signs, Mediums, and the Great Unknown

After losing Michael, I threw myself into reading everything I could on near-death experiences, theories of the afterlife, grief, and loss, and books written by mediums, people who claim to see and hear people who have died. It became like a second dissertation for me, to learn everything I could about this new world I believed my brother was a part of and to help me and my family cope with this life-changing reality and trauma. It also helped me feel more connected to my brother. I would read the books and, if they were any good, send a copy to my parents.

I remember my Aunt Linda watched a show by a medium by the name of John Edward, something about being able to hear from people who died. I went out and bought his book *One More Time*. I read it, and then we all read it. This became the first of many, many books we read on grief and loss. Some were written by mediums, some on near-death experiences, others by parents who also lost children or spouses. I listed several book recommendations in Chapter 12, "The Most Helpful Things We Did," if interested.

We saw a couple of mediums who were not very good, but when another mother who lost her son in Iraq as well referred us to Tim Braun, we hit the medium jackpot. With that said, maybe 70 percent of what he said made sense and was validating to us. Tim was trained by world-renowned medium James Van Praagh and was even more precise than John Edward.

Tim was a tall, thin, completely normal-looking guy in his thirties when we first met him, with a warm smile and kind eyes. His office was in a very generic, nondescript office. During a reading he looks over your shoulder, nodding and often saying "okay, okay," and then makes eye contact and deciphers what he hears and sees. He was able to describe what Michael looked like, his name, how he died, his age, his personality, all kinds of things. We didn't bring him a picture, give him a name, or tell him anything about him before we met Tim.

I have probably had half a dozen readings, and my parents went every six months for over ten years. In fact, Tim even included their story in one of his books, *Life and Death: A Medium's Messages to Help You Overcome Grief and*

Find Closure. These sessions feel like visits with Michael, although we can't actually hear or see him ourselves. We watched Tim interact with him, even laugh as he interpreted what he heard and saw, only asking, "Does that make sense to you? Do you understand this?" We felt validated that Michael's consciousness was still alive and it was also nice to know that Michael was aware of what was happening in our lives now.

For example, after my parents went on vacation to Hawaii, Tim said that he saw Michael placing leis on them. After my wedding, he asked if I got married and said Michael was wearing a tuxedo. You might be thinking, sure, anyone can look this up online or find this on social media. However, this was before Facebook, Instagram, and social media (hard to imagine, I know) and this information wasn't easily found online. Then there were the family dynamics he knew about that *most definitely* weren't online. One of my favorites was him saying that Aunt Linda had "the gift" (she is known to be a little bit of medium herself at times) and that people joked around that she was crazy. We couldn't believe he knew about that; nobody knew about that besides a few people in our family. My dad was quick to add that gift or no gift, she was definitely crazy. Despite all of the news articles written, I assure you *this* wasn't in any of them. My aunt did claim to hear from people who had already passed away at times (mostly her late husband) but it was not something we took very seriously and truthfully joked around about more than anything. My Aunt Linda's big hair, long nails and thick New York accent reminds me of the *Long Island Medium*. My aunt is definately one of my favorite kinds of crazy. And yes, she gave me her blessing to say this.

When we asked how Tim was able to hear from Spirit (as he would say), he explained to my family that he has to raise his "vibrations" or frequency and Spirit lower theirs, almost like tuning in to a radio station until you can hear the message. He would see images or feel feelings in his body he would have to make sense of and then ask if it made sense to us.

Michael wasn't the only person who came through in readings. Anyone you have lost can. So grandparents and other friends who have died have also come through over the years. Tim also asks at the end if we have any questions. Do I have any questions? I can ask questions all day long. And do in fact. One of the questions I asked was "What he is doing now?" This was many years ago, but Tim told us that he was helping other soldiers "cross over," and that he is with his fellow soldiers who also died in his unit, many of whom he sees in the readings as well. It gave us comfort to know he wasn't alone. He was with them, as well as my grandparents who have since passed.

Tim told me many times that I was going to write a book. I thought, *Oh no, I'm not writing a book. I don't know why he keeps saying that.* Well, we can see how that went. I will say it took over sixteen years before I sat down to write this; I hope they are patient over there on the Other Side, as Tim and other mediums call it.

The psychologist in me needs to be really clear here though: the sessions provide comfort and validation, but they do not replace or speed up the grief process. They don't bring your loved one back. However, it is a tool and for my family and me, a very helpful tool. I think for some parents especially and certainly mine, they *need* to know their child is okay and they will see them again. It is also very important to know that not all mediums have the same level of talent and skill. I saw several mediums who were far less skilled before we found Tim Braun. Some mediums can possibly make people feel worse if they don't hear from their loved one or give upsetting information. I would always recommend seeing a medium who has been referred to you. Also, Tim Braun recommends that you wait at least three months after someone has passed before having a reading.

Signs

In addition to seeing a medium, we learned from the books written by mediums, about how spirits try to communicate with us. I recommend James Van Praagh's book, *Talking to Heaven: A Medium's Message of Life After Death* on this topic. James discusses all the most common ways spirits try to connect with us, whether that be through music, electricity, animals, butterflies, hummingbirds, and even people to name a few. This is the language of energy.

Once we started to believe that Michael may be trying to give us "signs" that he is still around, we started paying a lot more attention to our surroundings and circumstances that others would write off as mere coincidence. We enjoyed sharing these different signs with each other. Many were around having the numbers forty-five or twenty-two come up, forty-five being his pager number in high school and twenty-two being the age when he died. Often music, too, such as songs coming on the radio that made us think of him, but one of the most unbelievable experiences or signs I had was in a small burger place near my house.

I want to start by saying that I love connecting with people; it's truly one of my very favorite things to do, but not just anywhere or anytime. I am not the "social butterfly" my mom admittedly loves to be. I get a lot of connection and time with my clients and with the people I am close to in my life, but I probably seem somewhat dismissive and guarded to people who don't know me. Not a huge fan of small talk with strangers. So when this man tried talking to me at Willie's Burgers, a corner restaurant near my home, I did everything to avoid this engagement. I really just wanted to get my breakfast burrito and leave. But he wasn't having it. At first he heard me talk to my daughter. "Oh my daughter's name is Mikayla too," he said.

"Oh really?" I commented. Nice, look away. My nonverbal body language showing little interest in talking right now.

"My son was in the Army in Texas," he went on to say.

Huh, I started thinking. "Oh wow, my brother was in the Army and did his advanced training in Texas too," I shared. Now I was slightly more interested. Was this a sign?

"His name is Michael Anthony," he said.

What?!! You can't make this up. That's my brother's first and middle name. *Wow, now you have my attention.* He was a pleasant man and I still remember his big, warm smile. My burrito was ready and I told him it was nice to meet him and left. I was so stunned. I walked away saying to myself, *Hi, Michael, I hear you! And quite the persistence!* Impressive.

If I hadn't nearly immediately wrote that down after it happened, I'm not sure that I would even believe this story years later. But it was a way for Michael to let me know he is still around and saying hello.

Another one-of-a-kind sign came in the form of a song one day in my office. I had a very challenging session involving a traumatic grief and loss case and in my head was wondering if I was going in the right direction. Out of nowhere my Pandora started playing, a Michael song, "Love Me When I'm Gone" by Three Doors Down. I didn't even know it was on. I was in a session and had to get up to shut it off. In the ten years I had been using Pandora at the office, this had never happened before and hasn't since. And of the thousands of possible songs, this one played? What are the chances? It just starts playing? On its own? I took it as a sign that Michael was telling me that I was on the right track and that he was there with me. This case involved the traumatic loss of my client's son, who died very unexpectedly, and was easily one of the hardest but most rewarding cases of my career.

If you want some signs from your sibling, ask for signs and be open. Does anything strange happen through electricity, music, animals, people? Will someone say a phrase that reminds you of your sibling? Be open and see what happens...

Dreams

If signs are the communication by day, then dreams are the visits at night. Over the years I have had many dreams with Michael in them. Some dreams that feel very real are called "visits" by mediums. This altered state of consciousness during our dream state allows us to be more open to such visits than in waking states. Apparently some people can even learn to do this in deep forms of meditation.

In many of my dreams, Michael was younger, maybe somewhere between eight to twelve years old. I remember knowing we were spending time together in the dream but that he wasn't alive in real life, wondering if he knew he had died since he didn't mention anything about it in the dreams. In one of my favorite dreams, however, he was older, around twenty-two, and we were playing cards together at my parents' kitchen table. My husband was there too and in the dream I realized that they had never met in real life, so I introduced them. "Michael, this is Josh. Josh, this is my brother, Michael," I said and they shook hands. This was a deeply meaningful moment for me and I can still picture it vividly from my dream because they never got to shake hands in real life. They knew of each other; Josh would overhear us talking on the phone and he knew we wrote letters back and forth while Michael was in boot camp and Iraq, but unfortunately, they never got to meet each other. I know they would have really liked each other. They both are adventurous and would have enjoyed doing things like snowmobiling and snowboarding together. It is yet another painful part of losing a sibling so young; they don't get to know your partner or your children.

My sister, Dani, also shared one of her most vivid dreams of our brother:

> *We were in the car. Michael was sitting in the front wearing a white sweatshirt as he always does in my dreams of him. I was sitting in the back and asked, "How are you doing?" And he was really calm and he said, "I'm good. I'm really good." I remember not understanding and asked him, "How can you be good? We aren't good, we are a mess. Don't you miss us?" And he said, "No, because there's no missing here but you can't understand it. I'm still with you but you won't understand that until you're here; there's no missing." I felt very much at peace and woke up feeling like I had just had a real "visit" from him.*

Even as I type this I am aware that some people might have an issue with this chapter and maybe even feel this shouldn't be in this book. I can hear my scientifically minded colleagues already: *Just a coincidence. You want to make everything be a sign. You want to believe all of these dreams are visits from your brother.* I believe that what the field calls "meaningful coincidences" are not really coincidences at all but rather events that happen on purpose. And here is my thinking...even if ninety-nine out of a hundred "signs" aren't, if I negate them all, I will miss the one in one hundred that really is a sign or hello from Michael. And I'm not willing to do that. I also think that talking about dreams, noticing signs, even seeing a medium were part of the grieving process for us.

Chapter 10

THE CHAPTER FOR THERAPISTS AND IDEAS TO BRING TO YOUR THERAPY

I think it was two years before I could mention my experience of losing my brother with clients. And over time I went to trainings on bereavement and eventually facilitated my own trainings on grief and loss. One of my specialties now is working with people with significant loss, such as the loss of a parent or sibling, loss of a child or grandchild, and loss of several family members at once. With these clients, when the time is appropriate, I do share about the loss of my brother. My experience of watching and helping my own parents with the loss of their son, and of understanding significant loss firsthand, has helped me with my clients. I see some of my clients for years, and their feedback has been that it helps for them to know about my personal experience with loss. I am able to show my clients that you can learn to live with such significant loss, even though when you first lose someone, you can't imagine how that is possible.

Therapy can be enormously helpful in navigating through the darkest days of losing a loved one, especially when the loss is significant and life-changing. Not only is your therapist trained to help you through very difficult feelings, but you don't need to worry that you will overwhelm them or that they will start avoiding you because you are "too much," "too down," or "too negative" these days, as you may fear your friends will start feeling. And truthfully, this may be too much for your friends and family to talk about all the time. The beauty of therapy is you can and should talk about and process these feelings for as long as you need to. That is their job.

You may need to talk about all of the messy feelings that accompany grief. Not just sadness but anger—anger at losing a sibling too soon, anger at your family sometimes for grieving differently than you or needing too much from you at times, possibly anger toward God or life in general. You may feel angry if your sibling took their own life. You may feel anger at your partner for not understanding what you are going through or anger at your closest friends who have always been there, yet fall short now when you need them the most. These are all feelings people experience at times, but saying them out loud is important and can help you process through some of the energy and hurt attached to those feelings. I spent many years in therapy after losing my brother, which I found invaluable, and now I help my clients with the array of complex emotions that grief and loss evoke. There are many layers to this loss; how this affects you as a person, as a family, and how it changes your present and future. If you had a challenging and difficult relationship with your sibling, their death may end the opportunity for that relationship to ever get better. This might be the most painful part for you. Therapy serves as a guide helping you navigate and sift through it all.

Finding the right therapist is important. Therapists all have different styles and specialties. I would first recommend trying to get a referral from a friend, doctor, or someone who has worked with this person before. It is not always easy to find someone who accepts your insurance, so keep that in mind. I believe therapy is one of the best and most important investments you can make in your life, and worth the cost. A good website to find a therapist in your area is www.psychologytoday.com. You can see people's profiles, pictures, specialties, and descriptions of how they work. If you have to use insurance, I would recommend you get a list from your insurance of therapists in your area and look them up on www.psychologytoday.com. If this all feels overwhelming, maybe ask someone to help you look through profiles and narrow down a few people to call. When you leave a message, I recommend you mention that you lost your sibling and are seeking grief and loss counseling. Therapists tend to get a lot of voicemails, and so the more clear and detailed your message, the better. Plus, if this is not their specialty or they don't have openings, hopefully they will call you back with some good referrals.

If you are a therapist, you may not currently specialize in grief and loss per se, but chances are during your career, you will have clients go through significant loss, of a child, sibling, spouse, or parent as a young person. For one, I recommend that you remember the name of the person they are grieving and use their name. I even ask if people would like to bring a picture of that person to therapy. I do this because I want the person to feel real to me because they are very real for your client. I would never refer or pressure your clients into talking about the loss; however, checking in with them is often very appreciated. They are used to society's quiet pull to keep moving along, not bringing up or checking in with them and "moving on." On the other hand, I believe that significant loss is something people move through and learn to live with.

Recognize that families and couples grieve differently. You might be one of the only people and my guess is you are one of a handful of people they can talk about their feelings with on this. A spouse who has never lost a sibling might not understand or be supportive enough. A spouse who doesn't want to talk about their feelings of losing a child as much as the other may leave your client feeling alone in their grief. Also the experience of the change in sibling dynamics should be explored. Maybe your client went from being the younger sister to an only child, or the middle child to the oldest. This is a very strange experience for someone and worth acknowledging and discussing.

I recommend exploring your clients' spiritual beliefs—where do they feel their loved one is now? Be aware of the anniversary of their loved one's passing and help explore what can be done to honor this, if a client wants to. Know that even seasons can be triggering, especially the holiday seasons and the season someone died in. We unconsciously remember the smells and lightning that occurs during that time and is often season specific.

Grief groups are often free and available in many areas. Some are open and address a mixture of different types of grief; others are more specific. Compassionate Friends is a group for parents who lost children, Friends for Survival is for people who lost someone to suicide, and I have seen several groups for widows. You may notice here that you didn't see a group for the loss of a sibling or twin. These groups are likely far and few between; sadly, I don't think I have seen any in my area on that. However, maybe they are in yours. I would Google that to find out.

Trauma therapies

If you are experiencing a lot of trauma symptoms, such as nightmares, flashbacks, feelings of numbness (which can also be a common grief symptom), and depersonalization (feeling that things aren't real, like you are in a movie or a dream), you may need to do a trauma modality such as EMDR (Eye Movement Desensitization Reprocessing) or CRM (Comprehensive Resource Model) in addition to regular talk therapy. These models help your brain process trauma faster than traditional psychotherapy can sometimes. If you also have childhood trauma, I would recommend you work with someone who does CRM, a newer, lesser known model than EMDR. If you have experienced trauma only as an adult, either CRM or EMDR could be good options for you. Sacramento-based trauma specialist Curtis Buzanski, MFT explains that CRM is more helpful with childhood trauma and dissociation, or "checking out" mentally or feeling detached from one's body, which often occurs during sexual abuse as a child. Just recalling the trauma can bring back a tendency to disassociate.

Depending on the severity of the trauma, or if I am finding that my work alone with clients is not reducing their trauma symptoms, I also have them begin seeing one of my colleagues who specializes in either EMDR or CRM. I have found that people benefit from both trauma work and having someone to talk to about everything else as well, family dynamics, relationship issues, work issues, struggles with self-care, etc. Referrals are always best but, depending on your area, can be hard to find. These are specialties that require additional training. To find a therapist who is trained in EMDR, go to www.emdria.org and for CRM, www.comprehensiveresourcemodel.com.

Since many people assume that therapy is covered by their insurance, I want to mention that in many, if not most cases, you will be referred to a therapist who does not accept insurance, or your particular insurance. It is very difficult in some areas (including the Sacramento and Bay Area) to find therapists with openings even paying their full fee. You can always ask to go on someone's waiting list or see if they offer a sliding scale.

My final pitch about therapy though is that it can be one of the best investments of your life. Not only can therapy help decrease levels of anxiety and depression but also forever improve your sense of self and your capacity to cope and understand your feelings, increase your self-awareness, and improve your relationships and parenting abilities. I think if you are a parent, one of the best gifts you can give your children is to do your own work. We raise our children from who we are, not just what we tell them or show them but what we embody and how we have made sense of our lives and the things we have gone through. Please seek help if you are struggling. This might be too much to navigate through alone.

Chapter 11

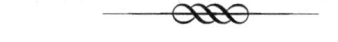

THE INTERVIEWS

When I first decided to interview others who had lost siblings, I thought it was to help give me ideas on what should be in this book, what others found helpful when they lost their sibling, what they wished had been in bereavement books, etc. However, I found their stories so powerful and moving, I had to share their experiences as well. What particularly struck me was that whether they had lost their sibling six months ago or sixteen years ago, they each spoke of their experience so intensely. They spoke of the profound impact losing their sibling(s) had on them and how connected to their sibling(s) they still are.

I realized that in reading this book, you may not identify with my story of loss, but you may with theirs, such as becoming an only child after losing your sibling, losing a twin, or having nobody left from your family of origin after your sibling(s) die. I interviewed fourteen people who lost siblings, five of whom lost not one, but two siblings. Their stories are powerful, candid, and with their permission, I am grateful to share them with you. Some of the names and information have been changed for privacy purposes. Some interviews were in person, others over the phone, as the interviewees are from all over parts of California and the country. Over the next two chapters, I will include some of the information they shared with me. The following are a few of the questions I asked and some of their responses.

What helped you in your grief process? And what made it worse?

Annie, 54, who lost her older sister—and only sibling—four years ago from a pulmonary embolism (blood clot in the lung) stated, *"The main thing that helps is knowing she isn't in pain anymore. She was in a lot of physical and psychological pain from a car accident. I believe she is in heaven and not in pain. Mostly, remembering all the good things she was, all the ways I was blessed to have her as a sister. When she passed, I went through all the feelings associated with loss, but at some point, something else happened; my heart, my love for all that she was completely opened up. I was able to finally see her so much more clearly without all of my judgment and preoccupation with boundary setting. There isn't anything in the way anymore and that is the blessing, that is what helps; the love grows even after she is gone. What doesn't help? Getting stuck in all of the regrets."*

Mark, 59, one of six siblings, lost his younger sister to breast cancer seven years ago: *"It helped to be able to talk about her, talk about her accomplishments. Really helped talking about her to other people. It helps me remember."*

Jill, 48, lost her sister seven years ago to a brain tumor (glioblastoma). *"Find your support whatever it is, therapist, family, self-care...but make time for that, fiction books, trips, ocean, exercise."*

Angela, 46, lost her younger sister nineteen years ago from a head trauma. Her response was *"Time...having a family of your own. I had a baby three years later and it helped start healing all of us, my parents and brothers. Something new to focus on, new exciting little blessing to focus on added hope to us all."*

When asked what made it worse, Angela responded, *"I didn't know anyone at that point that had suffered that kind of loss (sibling). I remember feeling very alone. People quickly go back to their lives, which I understand but I felt extremely alone. I didn't want to share this with my parents because of what they were going through."*

Tomei, 34, lost two brothers three years ago in a motorcycle accident, an older brother age 34 and a twin brother, 31. Her response was *"Questions were what made it worse for me. I hated all the questions. Some people didn't know they had died, and they would ask where my twin was, and it was just brutal to answer that question. Doing the things I used to do with my twin was hard, so I had to completely change up my routine...and to try and create my own identity, without (him). ...It was hard to lose my older brother. But* my twin was detrimental. I just completely lost who I was... he was my other half. My best friend."

Dani, 42, my sister, also shared, *"At first it hurts when people look at you with such pity and sadness and ask if you are okay. And then it hurts when that stops and nobody is asking anymore."*

I detail more about what helped people in the next chapter, "The Most Helpful Things We Did." However, before I move on, I'd like to address something that several people referenced. In a number of interviews, using substances too much to cope was brought up and how *"self-medicating with alcohol made it worse."* For added privacy, I won't be quoting people directly on this, but one person stated, *"Nothing helped in the first three years. I just partied. I just pulled away from everyone and focused more on 'party friends' because I didn't want to talk about it. I just numbed myself for a while."*

This is a similar sentiment to what a few others mentioned in the beginning as well. The first few weeks, months, and sometimes years of losing your sibling can be filled with darkness and feelings of intense sadness and a desire to "numb out" to feel less. I share this because again, if someone is reading this and can relate, please be careful with using substances to cope. I encourage you to reach out to others for support during this time. If you can't or don't want to talk to your family or friends, or that isn't helping enough, consider finding a therapist to help you with your grief. Another reminder that addiction can come in many forms: gambling, food, pornography. Seek help if you need to.

How have you changed from losing your sibling?

People answered this in many different ways. For those whose loss was more recent, in the last three years, their answers reflected the traumatic reactions you experience after losing someone unexpectedly.

Liz, 36, who lost her brother to suicide three years ago when he was thirty-nine, said, *"Now anytime family calls multiple times or at a different time, you immediately worry that someone else has died or something bad has happened, but that is diminishing."*

My experience, personally and professionally, is that this traumatic response and reaction does dissipate with time, but it can take several years, possibly more. It does tend to decrease in intensity and frequency over time.

Liz also shared how her expectations of others changed and shared that she *"learned to not hold it against people that can't talk about it, who haven't experienced significant loss. I was hurt in the beginning and felt they didn't care but now see it as a lack of understanding."* I think many times people wish they could be helpful but simply don't know what to say or do, so they often don't say anything. I will address this more later in the chapter on what to say or not say to grieving people.

Jesse, 43, discussed how losing her younger sister to breast cancer two years ago at the age of thirty-four changed her relationship with her parents. *"It really changed my relationship with my parents...It's complicated because you feel the need to comfort them while still going through the loss myself. I felt really bad for them, like their grief was worse."*

Raychel, 47, lost her older sister thirteen years ago to breast cancer, and her older brother in the last year to lung cancer. Raychel's parents have also died. So her brother was the last person from her family of origin. She expressed feeling like *"an orphan now, super untethered. Nobody left that knew (me) from the beginning, no family at our kids' functions. It's not supposed to happen this way. They were my biggest role models."*

What do you want people to know or understand about sibling loss?

Many of the siblings spoke about how significant the impact of losing their sibling was for them, as well as the need for more support.

Angela, 46, expressed, *"How truly hard it is. I wish people could have found time to keep reaching out, her friends, my friends; it all stopped too soon."*

Rolanda, 63, who lost two older brothers over seventeen years to diabetes and multiple myeloma, stated, *"They say the longest relationship you have in your life is with your siblings. You have known them your whole life; it's like losing a limb. You can go on without your arm but you lose a major part of you when you lose a sibling. They share your childhood memories, jokes, played games with, told secrets to, everything. Very unique relationship, unlike with your parents, spouse, that no one acknowledges."*

Mary, 39, lost her younger brother in a car accident fifteen years ago. *"That it is dynamic and constantly changing. It's deep and visceral and evolves over time. And it's okay to talk about it but I want to talk about the happy stuff. We need to create a dialogue about these things, a healthy remembrance."*

Jesse, 43, who lost her younger sister two years ago at the age of thirty-four to breast cancer, expressed, *"Way more sad than most people think it is. Really difficult...sometimes I feel guilty because I think about her more now since she is gone than when she was alive."*

Michelle, 41, lost her younger brother ten years ago to a violent crime. *"It never leaves you; it becomes a part of you. But it doesn't have to end you."*

Tomei, 34, expresses her experience of losing her twin brother three years ago by saying, *"A part of you dies; half of you is just gone. A very empty feeling, still feel lost and not whole. (Your twin) knows you best, you do everything with, you shared a language nobody else knew. We came out together and I expected to leave together."*

The theme of how one's relationship with one's sibling is different than any other relationship, considering so much shared history, came up a number of times.

Samantha, 26, one of five siblings who lost two siblings within the last year, stated, *"(It) feels like part of your soul has died in a way...loss of self is unacknowledged. Where is my place in the world? In my family? I had this team that is kind of...gone. You share something with these people you don't share with anyone else, your childhood, the same parents, same set of rules, like the same kingdom, same world you grew up in."*

When asked what she wants people to understand about sibling loss, Samantha also expressed, *"That the relationship with your sibling continues. They aren't gone from your life...Grief is your new way to love and to continue your relationship with this person."*

Annie, 54, who lost her older sister and only sibling, shared, *"Your sibling shares your childhood memories with you. They share your story and experiences like no one else ever can or will. They are a piece of home to you together or apart; you hear their voice and you are home. I remember thinking that I will always have her, so I will never be alone. I did not have a family of my own, and honestly I thought that was okay because I had her and her family. I also planned that she and I would care for our parents and share and support one another in our grieving when that time comes. It's not like being an only child where that is all you know. This is an instant, without any warning or time to prepare, you are alone."*

I appreciate Annie sharing this because her story and concerns are different than mine. I still have my sister, but I imagine many people reading this book may relate to now feeling like an only child and all that entails.

The focus and support primarily going to parents was also a topic raised by many of the people I spoke with.

Tomei, 34, went on to say, *"It impacts the siblings much in the same way as the parents. The difference is that the remaining siblings not only have to deal with their own grief,* but their parents become absent because they are grieving so badly. It's not the parents' fault at all...The parents' grief gives them a blind spot. And they can't see beyond their own grief...Everyone forgets that you lost someone too. Everyone asked how my parents were doing, but thought we were fine."

Rolanda, 63, stated, *"It's like the grief of sibling loss is not acknowledged in society. Nobody talks about it; it's all about the parents, the mom, how is your mom doing?"*

Mary, 39, lost her younger brother fifteen years ago and one of five siblings. *"I wanted people to ask about me but they didn't care about me or about how my brother and sisters were coping. They only asked about my parents."*

In summary, they wanted people to understand how life-changing and profound the loss of a sibling has been in their life. Siblings are referred to as the "forgotten bereaved" because I think as a whole the gravity of sibling loss is not understood. Parents are an easier and clearer focus; they are living everyone's nightmare, to lose a child. Everyone, including the siblings in many cases, is focused on helping them, but this often leaves the sibling bereavers feeling alone, under supported, and lost in the process.

How long did it take to feel better?

I included this question because I know some people reading this might want to know when they will start feeling better again. I know I wondered that same question when I lost my brother, so I asked. However, this isn't an easy question to answer. In fact, I asked this in part to see what people's reactions would be—which often was a chuckle, and they wondered out loud how to answer that. The truth is you change so much. The physical pain you feel in your body, the shock, feeling like you are living in a fog, being unable to concentrate—all diminish in time. It might take a year, maybe two or three years, depending on how you lost your sibling or your relationship with them. If you lost your sibling slowly, over time to an illness, a "longer goodbye" might be experienced differently than if your sibling was killed suddenly, such as in a car accident or by suicide. These of course are rough estimates. The important thing to know is that you won't always feel the way you do in the beginning.

Angela, 46, who lost her younger sister nineteen years ago, stated, *"It's a process. But truly it felt better having my daughter three years later. The first year of holidays and birthdays was the worst, so difficult, second set a little easier...it really does get better and I couldn't and didn't believe that at the moment. The grief was unbearable."*

Tomei, 34, who lost her twin brother and older brother three years ago, stated, *"I am still going through the process, but I would tell other siblings that have lost their brothers or sisters to find a therapist that you connect with. My therapist is the only reason I and my other two siblings are standing here today. Don't wait for your parents to feel better. I am still struggling, but every day I feel just a little bit better. Sometimes a holiday or life event will put me back a few steps, but I just stay to my routine and keep making plans and never isolate."*

When people ask you how many siblings you have, how do you answer?

I asked this question because I know this can be a particularly difficult question to be asked after losing a sibling. I discussed this more in chapter six, "The Dreaded Questions." On one hand it doesn't feel right to not include your sibling who died, but it also doesn't feel right to tell your story to whoever may ask. Often this question is asked innocently, without someone realizing the land mine they unintentionally walked into.

My sister, Dani, age forty-two now but twenty-six when we lost Michael, was also one of the people I interviewed. Her response was *"Depends how I felt in the moment. I used to hate that question; it made me so uncomfortable. If you are single, it's really hard to accept that you are going to have a partner that has never known your sibling. And with dating, people ask you all the time how many siblings you have. Very hard in the beginning."*

Dani told me that she actually stopped telling people about Michael while she was dating. It felt too personal and vulnerable to talk about it when first dating someone. I also talk about this idea to clients, about who has earned the right to know their story. It is private, vulnerable, and yours to tell on your time. I also found from these interviews that people who lost their siblings more recently struggled and hesitated more with this question. They were more likely to not include their siblings when people asked because it still felt too awkward, too uncomfortable for everyone involved. However, those who lost their siblings more than five years ago answered quickly and without hesitation; their siblings were included.

Tomei, 34, who lost two brothers three years ago, stated, *"I say I have four but now I have two. I always preface that I do not know how to answer that question yet."*

Jill, 48, mentioned earlier from a family of five siblings, lost her sister seven years ago to a brain tumor (glioblastoma), and an older brother died before she was born. Jill currently has two living brothers, and answers the question this way: *"I say five and two are gone, or there were five and now there are three."*

Rolanda, 63, who lost two of her siblings and is the youngest of eight, answered, *"I always say I have seven siblings and there were eight children altogether."*

Melissa, 38, lost her brother twenty-two years ago when he was twenty-five and she was sixteen after an accident on their family farm. Melissa was the youngest of three and responded to the question, *"I always say I have two older brothers, or one of three and my oldest brother died."*

For myself, I often answer that I have a younger sister and lost my brother when he was twenty-two. However, it also depends on the context and the relationship I have with who is asking. I will say this though—this question does get easier over time.

What would you want people to say and NOT to say to you when they learned you lost your sibling?

The truest statement here is that most people do not know what to say to someone after they have experienced significant loss, but really wish that they did know what to say. People want to offer comfort, hope, and words that will feel helpful and healing. Unfortunately, people's comments can end up often being the opposite, causing hurt and anger. The other difficult reality about this question is that what is comforting and okay with one person does not feel reassuring to another. So, no right answer? Correct. However, the interviews provided several good examples of what people didn't like and what they *did* appreciate from others when they lost their sibling(s).

Melissa, 38, who lost her older brother when she was sixteen years old, said, *"I hated when people said 'I'm so sorry for your loss...' Don't say anything because there are no words. Just give them a hug. Look them in the eye and give them a hug."*

Others didn't mind hearing the standard "I am sorry for your loss" but noted that how it was said, if it felt genuine and authentic, mattered. Others liked comments such as, "I'm thinking about you."

Samantha, 26, who lost her younger brother less than a year ago to suicide and sister in a car accident within the same year, didn't like comments that felt judgmental, such as *"'I thought you would be crying more' and 'you look really good' because I was still wearing makeup or doing my hair. Also comments like 'be grateful for the time you had with them' or 'you'll get over it' were not helpful and felt minimizing of how huge the loss is. Comments that weren't judgmental or required a response felt better, such as, 'It's really good to see you. I'm thinking about you. I am sorry for your loss.'"*

A couple of people, when asked what people can say, answered that people can ask about them. Ask about their siblings. Ask their names.

Raychel, 47, lost her older sister thirteen years ago to breast cancer and her older brother four months ago to lung cancer. *"I love when people ask me about my siblings. It's really healing. I don't like pretending it didn't happen."*

Mary, 39 stated, *"I really like when people ask me his name. Now I always ask someone's name when I hear they died."*

Angela, 47, said simply, *"Listen, don't give your opinion. Offer a hug."*

Annie, 54, stated, *"Validating comments, such as 'That's a significant and devastating loss. I'm here for you if you want to talk or if you don't want to talk about it and need a break from the grief.' Hearing stories or memories about your sibling, you love hearing stories about them. I didn't like hearing things where people were trying to help you make some kind of sense out of it. The truth is untimely death does not make sense. It steals plans, hopes, holidays, Saturday afternoon movies, shopping for new shoes, raising kids, and everything in between. It leaves a hole you just learn to live with, but a piece of you remains broken. When people share their loss and are able to understand yours and the wreckage death leaves, that helps.*

One of the biggest mistakes people make is to assume if someone comes from a large family or has several other living siblings that it is less painful to lose one of them. Also, comments referencing God and infamous comments such as "God only gives people what they can handle" can feel painful and minimizing of one's loss.

Rolanda, 63, who lost two of her brothers and was the youngest of eight, did not like when people made comments such as *"Thank God you have a big family, so many brothers and sisters"* and *"God only gives you what you can take."*

In summary, it's probably best you don't speak for God, no matter how religious you are. It isn't your place and especially if it implies God did this because someone could "handle it." Some people feel betrayed by God after losing someone they love, especially if that person was quite young when they died. Again, you don't want your well-intentioned comments to leave someone feeling worse.

Another common question people will often get asked after losing someone is "Are you okay?" Most people are far from okay after losing a sibling. Pretty safe to say, stay away from this line of questioning.

A heartfelt hug or act of service or kindness such as bringing over food or flowers is likely a safer way to let someone know you care and are thinking of them and their loss. There are no perfect words, and unfortunately even with good intentions, the wrong choice of words can be hurtful. I trust that people don't mean to be hurtful, but rather, just don't know what to say. Unfortunately, one of the best teachers of this is by going through a similar loss. Depending on your relationship with someone, if you are reading this and want to know how to best support them, maybe just ask, "How can I best support you during this time?" And when in doubt, "thinking of you" and small gestures of food or flowers will probably land softly and feel thoughtful and meaningful.

The Gifts Left Behind

Not all the change that comes from losing a sibling is bad. That might feel impossible to believe in the beginning, but some of the people I know who have lost siblings have ended up living almost enhanced or enlightened lives. Borrowing Brené Brown's term, I see bereaved siblings frequently being "overfunctioners." They live very full lives, even when they are tired, down, and depressed. They keep pushing; they keep showing up for people they care about and things they believe in. You don't take time or relationships for granted anymore; instead they are prioritized. Some even feel they need to live for their lost sibling, do the things they can't do.

You get really in touch with what is most important, and I truly think this is a gift. For myself, I believe that I prioritize relationships and spending time with the people I care about. I don't take time for granted. I view opportunities as "windows" that will close someday and know to choose wisely, i.e., volunteering in my kids' classrooms, going on their field trips, working part time and making less money so that I can pick them up from school a couple of days a week. I am grateful I chose to visit my uncle several times and had quality time together before he died. I cherish those memories. Life is tough and it is hard to do and be everything we want to, but I believe it is about balance and essentially, balancing our priorities. Once some of the windows close, they can't be reopened. We need to choose what we do with our time and energy thoughtfully.

I am a more spiritual person since losing my brother. I believe we are here to learn important lessons and see life as a gift. I even try to embrace aging and that with every birthday, I "get to" turn another year older, because clearly, not everybody does. This is an ideal that I try to embrace, but that isn't to say that I don't have my moments of wanting to freeze or slow down the aging process of course.

I also believe one of the greatest ways to honor our siblings and loved ones is to live life differently, better and wiser, because of them. Through loving and losing them, it helps us focus on what is most important, and to live the rest of our lives differently because of them is truly powerful. I asked everyone this question, "What were some of the gifts left behind from losing your sibling? How has your life or perspective changed in a positive way?" It was tougher for the people who lost their siblings more recently, but here are some of their responses.

The reference to "not sweating the small stuff" came up in multiple interviews.

Jesse, 43, who lost her sister, 34, to breast cancer two years ago, expressed how losing her sister *"puts things in perspective, I don't sweat the small stuff. Our time here is short. I'm less held back from taking risks."*

Angela, 46, who lost her sister nineteen years ago to a head trauma, stated, *"She was very involved in giving back to the community, loved to help people, give back, joyful. I did sweat the small stuff. I worried and was angry about small things. That all shifted tremendously for me since she passed. I don't think I would be as involved with things as I am (in the community). I feel like I live for her and I."*

Empathy & a New Perspective on Life

Mark, 59, who lost his younger sister seven years ago to breast cancer, expressed, *"I look at life differently. Life is short and we never know how short it is going to be. There's no reason to save the good wine. I don't want to save things. I want to live every ounce I can live...taking the risks I never would have thought to do. I don't let the smaller things in life bother me as much. I look at things through a different lens, a softer lens, not so black and white. Who am I to judge people?"*

Jill, 48, who lost her sister to a brain tumor seven years ago, answered, *"Having more empathy for people. You never know what people are going through. Now I wonder when people are snappy or rude what they have been going through in the background."*

Gratitude, Faith & More Time with Family

Michelle, 41, who lost her younger brother ten years ago when he was the victim of a violent crime, expressed, *"I have more gratitude for still being here. Prioritizing relationships, greater appreciation of the family I do still have left. I try not to waste time and fix what I want to fix, what's important. I'm more thoughtful of who I let in my life."*

Rolanda, 63, who lost two brothers, discussed how her remaining five siblings spent more time together, started doing sibling dinners together, and are more expressive with each other after losing their two brothers. She discussed how they are all more connected now.

Annie, 54, who lost her older sister and only sibling four

years ago, moved in with her mother to help her heal from the loss. Her father passed away years ago. She shared, *"I never saw this coming, never conceived of it, I moved out at seventeen. After my sister passed, I went to stay with my mother. I came to deeply appreciate this time and see it for the priceless gift it is. I ended up staying because getting to really know your mother as an adult is incredible. I get all the life stories, not just the things you talk about over lunch or during a holiday. I know my mother now and understand her in ways I never had. We have a great relationship, and all of the things we are doing make up for all the things we didn't. It is such a great honor and source of peace for me to be in a position to keep her aging happily and comfortably at home."*

Raychel, 47, who lost both her older brother and sister to cancer, stated, *"Look at life for each moment that it offers me and living that. (I am) so very close to my nephews (her sister's sons) and so happy when they are around."*

Tomei, 34, one of five siblings and lost two brothers, stated, *"(I) found faith through all this...much closer now with siblings and family. I'm the oldest now. I get to boss everyone around."*

Dani, 42, my sister, expressed, *"A sense of spirituality and being connected to life after death, what is most important in life...teach my kids about spirituality through talking about Uncle Michael with them."*

When asked about the gifts left behind or any positive changes they made in their lives as a result of losing their siblings, the prioritizing of time, relationships, and gratitude came up over and over in the interviews.

Angela, 46, who lost her younger sister, stated, *"Definitely makes me realize that life is super short, live every moment, prioritize time and relationships."*

Melissa, 39, who lost her older brother twenty-two years ago, stated, *"Being grateful for our lives and all we have. Not take things for granted, not be afraid to express our love for each other. Our family is closer and helped us slow down, take vacations. My parents travel way more now than they ever did and I think that is a direct impact from my brother. Our motto is: Take the trip. And that really stems from what Chris would say, take the fuckin' trip."*

Traveling more is definitely something my family has done as well. Every year around Michael's birthday, we take a trip together as a family. I know for many years his friends would do camping trips around his birthday also. It feels better to honor people we miss and love. It feels better to change, honor them, and celebrate them. One of my favorite examples of change and honor comes from my father's first and only tattoo after losing Michael, which reads, "In Loving Memory of My Son, Michael." My dad wasn't a tattoo kind of guy, and Michael had several. I would have loved to see the look on his face when my dad did that for him!

I also enjoyed hearing about the different ways that people have honored their siblings and stayed connected to them over the years. One especially unique example was from Mark, 59, who lost his sister to breast cancer when he was fifty-two and she was fifty. Mark was the second of six children, and Pam, being the third of six, was the closest sister in age to him. His sister was cremated and their mother made jewelry for all the siblings to hold a small amount of her ashes. Mark was given a small tube with his sister's name on it. Mark is also a lifelong skydiver with nearly 6,000 jumps in the last twenty-seven years. In life, they jumped together twice. Since she has died, Mark described how his sister *"has done nearly 2,000 skydives with me"* tucked in his jumpsuit. A truly unique way of staying connected to his sister for sure!

Siblings have a deep need to keep their siblings close and to stay connected. The following chapter, "The Most Helpful Things We Have Done," is accumulation of the many things that were done to help with our grieving process and in many cases, ways to honor and remember our siblings. I hope some of these ideas feel helpful and inspiring to you as well.

Chapter 12

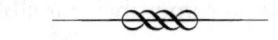

―⦅⦆―

The Most Helpful Things We Did

This chapter combines my ideas, as well those of my sister, my parents and from the interviews of fellow sibling bereavers. These were some of the most helpful things we did to heal and cope during the hardest parts of grieving. They don't go in any particular order.

Grief books: I read a lot of grief books by other people who had lost a loved one, yet only one on sibling loss since that was all I could find at the time. I read several books on the loss of a child, on near-death experiences, different theories about the afterlife, as well as books by mediums.

Our book recommendations:

Surviving the Death of a Sibling: Living Through Grief When an Adult Brother or Sister Dies by T.J. Wray

I Wasn't Ready To Say Goodbye: Surviving, Coping and Healing After the Sudden Death of a Loved One by Brook Noel & Pamela Blair, PhD

When There Are No Words: Finding Your Way to Cope with Grief and Loss by Charlie Walton (written by a father who lost two children)

Love Never Dies—A Mother's Journey from Loss to Love by Sandy Goodman

It's OK That You're Not OK: Meeting Grief and Loss in a Culture That Doesn't Understand by Megan Devine (Samantha, 26, and Jesse, 43, both recommended this book)

Getting Grief Right: Finding Your Story of Love in the Sorrow of Loss by Patrick O'Malley and Tim Madigan (written by a therapist who lost his infant son, also Samantha's recommendation).

One Last Time by John Edward (medium)

Talking to Heaven: A Medium's Message of Life After Death by James Van Praagh

Life and Death: A Medium's Messages to Help You Overcome Grief and Find Closure by Tim Braun

Therapy: As mentioned in chapter ten, seeing a therapist can provide a safe and confidential place to talk about your loss and the deep impact it has on many, if not all, parts of your life. Therapists all have different styles, so you may need to meet with more than one to see who you are most comfortable with. If you continue having nightmares, flashbacks, or other trauma symptoms, you may also want to consider doing EMDR (Eye Movement Desensitization Reprocessing) or CRM (Comprehensive Resource Model). Referrals are always best; however, www.psychologytoday.com is a great resource for reading therapists' profiles and finding someone in your area. For myself and many of the people I interviewed, therapy was a very helpful part of our grieving process. Michelle, 41, expressed, *"I didn't know anybody in my life that had lost a sibling. It completely shattered me. Therapy...was one of the only places or persons I could talk to."*

Writing in a journal: Journaling your feelings can be a great way to help process all of the mixed emotions you are experiencing. I wrote in a journal for a long time. I often wrote to my brother, telling him things I wanted him to know. Some people believe people who have passed away can hear our thoughts, so this was my way to try to communicate with him. I also kept track of all of the "signs" I would see so that I didn't forget them in time.

Having "Michael time": It helped in my grief process to have time designated just to grieve and connect with my brother. Sometimes I would play music that reminded me of him, talk to him, imagine what he would say back, or write to him. I have recommended this idea of having dedicated "sibling time" to my clients as well, where they make time for this purpose. They seem to really like and embrace this idea also.

Telling your story: Talking about my brother with my family was definitely a part of us not only grieving but keeping Michael's memory alive. We also would share the various signs we had from him. Liz, 36, mentioned how it helped to *"tell the story; I needed to process that it was real."* Many of the people I interviewed talked about how talking about their sibling with their family, friends, and therapists helped significantly in their grief process.

Talking to other people who lost siblings: Liz, 36, also said, *"It helps talking to others that lost siblings...it is reassuring that you will be okay, eventually."* Unfortunately, nobody understands this kind of grief other than somebody who has already experienced the loss of a sibling.

Starting a foundation: When my father saw the flowers pour in early on, he wanted to create a way to further honor my brother's life and death, and began asking for donations in lieu of flowers. We ultimately created the Michael A. DiRaimondo Foundation. My father organized golf and poker tournaments, with the help from many others. This helped us have something to focus on, do together and grow, as a way to help cope during those first several years. We ended up raising $250,000 for the foundation and award a $10,000 scholarship to send one person to paramedic school annually.

Exercise: I didn't even like running before losing Michael, but I ran a lot in those first years after his death. I put on music that reminded me of him or music that helped get me in the zone. It became a way to have "Michael time" and work through my grief. Exercise also raises our levels of serotonin, dopamine, and endorphins—neurotransmitters that naturally help us have a sense of well-being and lower anxiety and depression. Not to mention exercise helps provide a plethora of health benefits to our body and brain. I highly recommend exercising on a regular basis, even if that means just going on walks. You can always start with a short walk, fifteen to twenty minutes, and build from there. (Of course consult with your physician before beginning an exercise program.)

Yoga: Samantha, 26, and Tomei, 34, both lost two siblings and mentioned how yoga helped them through their grief. Tomei talked about how the structure of going to yoga classes three or four times a week helped her not fall apart and *"surrender to the sadness."* Samantha mentioned dedicating her practice to her siblings.

Music: Samantha also connected to her brother and sister through both listening to their Spotify playlists as well as making a playlist that reminded her of each of them. *"Music is huge for me,"* she expressed as one way to help with her grieving process and a way to feel connected to her siblings.

Painting: My sister, Dani, found painting on canvases helpful. Although she painted a variety of things, she often painted lotuses. I love her paintings and still have two of them up in my home to this day.

Crying: Mary, 39, lost her brother and stated that *"crying and releasing the emotions felt very helpful. It helped to lift the weight of the grief."*

Nature: It felt really peaceful and healing to spend time in nature. I remember snowshoeing in Lake Tahoe, where I got the idea to name my future daughter, Mikayla, after Michael. Nature and its beauty felt bigger than me and my grief, like it embraced me and provided peace.

Out of the Darkness Walk: Liz, 36, who lost her brother to suicide when she was thirty-three and he was thirty-nine, found the suicide awareness fundraiser "Out of the Darkness Walk" very helpful. She discussed this as *"a really good way to honor and remember them."* In addition to suicide, if you lost your sibling to a health condition such as cancer, participating in an organized walk and fundraiser may be worth trying at least once.

Start a garden: Raychel, 47, who lost her sister when she was thirty-four and brother when she was forty-seven, planted gardens for both of them in their honor. She believes irises are a sign from her sister.

Travel: This goes along with nature for me. I remember going to Ireland and at first worried I would feel so far away from my brother, since it was a place he had never been to. Instead, I felt empowered by the beauty of Ireland and amazed and relieved about how connected I still felt to Michael there. It helped me realize that I could feel him anywhere, no matter where I went. It wasn't about the location per se. I was the connection.

Facebook and social media: My sister and I post pictures and a message for Michael on the anniversary of his passing (Jan 8th), Memorial Day, and his birthday (June 2nd) on Facebook and Instagram. We receive many posts from friends, family, and his friends with expressions of love, support, and remembrance. It truly helps seeing everyone's engagement and messages. To know others also love and remember your sibling means the world to those grieving. Plus, I think it gives everyone else who loves and misses your sibling an opportunity to participate, which is healing for them as well. Rolanda, who lost two brothers, has a tradition of playing her brothers' favorite songs on Facebook every year on each of their birthdays.

Read the Bible and pray: If you are a prayerful person, I would recommend praying to God, the Universe, whatever you connect with. Ask for help, support, and guidance. Annie, who lost her sister when she was forty-nine, shared that reading the Bible and her relationship with God was a big part of her healing process. She expressed, *"We are not here for ourselves, and everything is a blessing. The challenging and even devastating experiences are molding us into the best versions of ourselves. I talk to Him (God) all the time. So guess what, I'm not alone."*

Asking for signs: My sister, Dani, would ask for specific signs from Michael when she wanted to know he was present. A powerful example of this is when her daughter, Natalie, was born with a heart defect that required her to have open heart surgery at two weeks old. While at the hospital, Dani asked to see someone in fatigues as a sign from Michael that Natalie would be okay and that he was there with her. An Army shirt or a flag wouldn't do; it *had* to be fatigues. For the sign to "count," it had to be something unlikely to happen. After a couple of hours, sure enough a man walked by in complete military fatigues right outside the waiting room of a children's hospital in Los Angeles. My sister even took a picture to hold on to this sign. Thankfully, the surgery was a success and Natalie is a bright-eyed, healthy five-year-old little girl now who is a ball of energy, personality, and joy.

Cultural Memorials: Unless your sibling was in the military, American culture does not have an annual day to memorialize our loved ones. We may need to borrow ideas from other cultures and religions. Jill, 48, honors her sister, whom she lost to a brain tumor when her sister was forty-three and she was forty-one, by making a shrine for her on Dia de los Muertos, a Latin American holiday which means, Day of the Dead. This is celebrated every year from October 31st to November 2nd. Every year, Jill puts out *"pictures, food she would like, a glass of wine for her and talk about Aunt Jennifer."* Her children participate in this annual tradition as well, which I think is a meaningful way to teach our children how to also honor our siblings and family members who have passed.

Seeing a medium: I know this idea is likely the most controversial on this list and I understand that it isn't the right choice for everyone. However, it might be for you and it was for my family. With that said, seeing a medium is only one of the many things we did in our grief journey. If you are interested in seeing a medium, it is very important you see someone who comes highly recommended to you. There are many mediums who are not highly skilled and could make you feel worse. I do recommend the medium we saw many times, Tim Braun. www.timbraunmedium.com.

Chapter 13

THE GRIEVING PROCESS IN OTHER CULTURES AND RELIGIONS

    As a Catholic-raised, third-generation Italian-American, my experience with grief was very Americanized. Meaning, we had a wake the night before the funeral, which is a smaller service than the funeral and an opportunity for people to speak and provide condolences to the family. This is also an opportunity for people to say their good-byes to a loved one. Then came the funeral, which was held at our local Catholic church, and this was open to the public and a significantly larger service with nearly a thousand people. After that, there are no further memorial services or traditions in the Catholic or American grieving process. Given that my brother was in the military, we also honor him on Memorial Day. But many don't have that. This limited grieving process is similar across many Christian denominations. Catholics, Protestants, and others all traditionally hold funerals within the week of one's death, and some have wakes the day before or have small services at the gravesite, but many of them don't have any traditions beyond that. It should be noted that Eastern Orthodox Christians do have a forty-day mourning period along with memorials at six months, one year, and three years after a loved one's death.

Mainstream American culture—and in particular, many Christian faiths—don't have other rituals or traditions that aid in the grieving process, making the experience harder. This leaves people without a map or guide to not only *get through* but also learn how to *live with* grief. In contrast, other countries and religions do. In fact, one example that comes to mind is the Mexican holiday, Dia de los Muertos, or Day of the Dead. This holiday is celebrated from October 31st to November 2nd every year in Latin American countries to remember and honor their deceased family members. This is a time that gravestones are visited and cleaned up, altars are decorated with pictures and flowers, and favorite meals are made for the deceased. This helps not only individuals but families memorialize and honor their loved ones every year as it is part of their community and cultural tradition.

Buddhism is the fourth largest religion in the world and the predominant religion in a number of countries, including but not limited to China, India, Sri Lanka, Japan, Thailand, Cambodia, Vietnam, and Malaysia. Annual memorials for loved ones are also part of the Buddhism religion. These memorial services are held either on the anniversary of a loved one's death or near the time of their death.

I have learned a lot about how other cultures and religions grieve from my clients and friends. In the Japanese culture, the majority of memorial services follow Buddhist practices. Therefore, a service is held when a person first dies, then again after forty-nine days, one hundred days, one year later, three years, five years, and seven years. This nearly perfectly matches how people grieve and what helps them in their grief process. At first people are usually in such shock or grief, they can barely remember the funeral or services. You can hardly remember who was there, what was said to you, or what was said during the services. The whole thing feels like a blur, which is why I actually recommend you have people take pictures and/or videotape the services so you can watch another time. At a minimum, have people print out what they say if they speak at the services.

By forty-nine days, you are actually ready for a service because usually people have gone back to their lives and you are still grieving. This way people come back together and you get an opportunity to get support, honor your loved one, and grieve together. At one hundred days, same thing. The one-year anniversary is symbolic of marking time, making it through a full year and often very painful for people. In American culture, there is no specific tradition to have a memorial, so again people often do this alone. Three years, five years, and seven years are important markers for most significant loss, and opportunities to receive the support you need and to grieve *as a family and community* versus alone.

In addition to actual services, some cultures and religions have rules or traditions for how people can or should dress or behave in the beginning of their grief. My understanding is that many years ago, Italian women would wear black for a year after their husbands died. Another tradition was for mourners to only wear black for the first forty days, then again at one year. It was seen as disrespectful to wear colors. No celebrations of major events or dancing were done for one year. I think these are helpful traditions for several reasons. For one, wearing all black is a good reminder to others that someone is grieving and needs support and/or understanding in a difficult time. And one of the hardest things for people in deep grief to do is participate in celebrations, parties, or large gatherings for a while. This is taken off the table and they are not expected to participate.

In Judaism, there are five stages in the mourning process over the first years after a loved one's death. Shiva, which is considered the third stage, begins after the funeral and lasts for seven days. During this time immediate family member discuss their loss and receive support from extended family members and the community in the form of meals and emotional support. Traditionally, people would cover their mirrors for thirty days so that the focus was more on grieving and not one's appearance. Also people would come over to comfort the family every day for thirty days. The anniversary of their loved one's death, known as Yahrzeit, is honored every year in one's home. A Yahrzeit candle is lit at sunset of the anniversary and stays lit for twenty-four hours. Some people also participate in fasting, study the Torah, visit the gravesite, and donate to charity on behalf of their loved one.

The candles are also lit on the Jewish holidays, Passover and Yom Kippur, in remembrance of loved ones.

These are just a few examples of how other countries and religions have detailed and extended memorial services and bereavement practices to honor and remember loved ones and help people with the grieving process; there are many others as well. As you can see, this is much different than my experience and many others outside of these religions. I can see how these traditions help significantly and how without them, many people feel quite alone in their grief after the funeral is over, and everybody goes back home and returns to their lives. I don't know what the answer is. Should mainstream America adopt some of these cultural traditions? Should we have our own version of Dia de los Muertos? I wish we did and think that would be a good start.

I include this chapter because I think it matters how the grieving process works elsewhere and how it has been handled in the past. I also include this information to further validate how challenging grieving can be, especially when support and traditions are limited. Other bereavement customs continue throughout the first year, certainly well beyond the funeral, and people annually memorialize their loved ones to help facilitate the grieving process. I also believe this helps normalize the experience of remaining connected to your loved ones, even in death. It helps people continue their relationships with these loved ones, even if they are no longer physically here. If you are not part of a culture or religion that has these customs, maybe you adopt one that resonates with you. Maybe this means participating in Dia de los Muertos or having a small service or gathering of close friends and family on the anniversary of their passing, or a memorial day where you honor all the loved ones who have passed. These are ideas worth considering. It helps us to be around other people who also loved our siblings, miss them, and can share stories about them with us. These ongoing memorials and services provide such opportunities.

When Someone Doesn't Want a Funeral

In my practice, I have heard of all different types of funerals, services, and celebrations of life. But I have also heard about people respecting a loved one's wishes to not have anything done after their death. However, these events are just as much, if not more, for your loved ones left behind, still living. This is especially true for American culture, which has very few traditions and rituals for grief and loss. It is really important to have a way to not just grieve privately, but as a group as well. Whether this is a funeral in a church, or a small gathering by a river, the event details matter less. The act of honoring your loved one is, in my professional opinion, a very important and helpful part of the grieving process.

The families and individuals I have seen that didn't have any services for their loved one seem to lack a formality in their grief process, almost like unfinished business. They are conflicted between wanting to respect their loved one's wishes but are left with a deep feeling and question of whether enough was done to honor them at the same time. So although people sometimes tell their families that they don't want a fuss made after their death, I would encourage people to let their loved ones decide what to do, because not doing anything can actually hinder the grieving process. It isn't about you, and yet all about you at the same time. Grief is a complex and layered experience. However, typically the more support one receives, formal and informal, public and private, the more healthy the grieving process.

I include this because my hope is that this book helps people understand grief, loss, and grieving in a different way. Maybe you are reading this as someone who thought they didn't want services done for them or has a parent who says that. I hope you consider this suggestion, because like many important times in life, this is a window of opportunity. You can memorialize someone later but you don't usually have a funeral years later. Your parents would likely want what is best for you, or you would want to do what is best for your loved ones.

The Final Chapter

My Wish

Let's change how we grieve. I want to be a part of changing how people are encouraged to grieve in this country. One of my favorite ways social media is used is when I see people honor their loved ones who have passed. Every year my sister and I create posts with pictures on the anniversary of my brother's passing, Memorial Day, and his birthday. I think it is not only a helpful outlet for us, as we get support, comments, and reactions we truly appreciate, but I also think it is a healthy and positive experience for Michael's friends, our cousins, and other family members to express their grief as well. This is living with grief. We don't get over or move on from some loss; we change, we live with it, we live with the missing, and we honor them along the way.

I love how we have integrated my brother into our family. All of the four grandchildren know of their Uncle Michael, refer to him by name, have included him in their family tree for school projects (with an angel sticker), and talk about him in school around Memorial Day; he is an integral part of their, and our, family story. My daughter, Mikayla, is named after him. My son, Mason, has the number "45" on his go-kart for competitive racing in honor of Uncle Michael, since forty-five is a number that has been associated with my brother in many ways before and after his death.

Michael died before I was even married, so neither my husband nor children ever met him. But just because he isn't physically here doesn't mean he isn't here. He is present in many other ways. We might have lost our siblings and loved ones physically, but it doesn't end our relationships with them. We very much still feel connected emotionally, psychologically, and spiritually. And we can continue to have them be a meaningful part of our families and our family stories. If that feels right to you, I encourage you to do so.

My wish is that this book has helped my fellow sibling bereavers feel more understood and validated in their feelings and experiences, and have more ideas on how to navigate through these difficult and painful times. I also hope this book has offered some ideas on how to honor your brother or sister or help others understand what you are going through.

What I look forward to, many, many years from now (hopefully), is to see my brother in the afterlife, give him a huge, long hug, and talk about all that we have been through. I want to know about his feelings and experiences, what the heck he has been doing this whole time, and what he thought of all we did for him. That will be a beautiful, long-awaited moment. I can picture it now. I imagine some reading this would feel very similar.

But for now, we wait, all still living without them physically here. We live with the missing. We hold on to the invisible thread, that unbreakable connection, and we honor them, love them, talk about them, and do our best, living with grief. Because it is the best we can do. One moment at a time, one day at a time, and sometimes, one breath at a time.

Epilogue

The human spirit is incredible. We love so intensely and, as a result, hurt and grieve even more intensely. I believe we all have powerful stories of loss. I truly do not believe there are enough resources, groups, books, or podcasts about grief and loss, especially sibling loss. We need each other's stories; human beings are by nature storytellers. We need to hear the untold stories of the loss of a twin, sibling, or whatever your story is. I encourage you to consider sharing your story whether that be in the form of writing a book, starting a podcast, or attending a bereavement group. We have so much to learn from each other, and in the process, it can help us all heal from this incredibly painful experience.

At the core of the human experience, we want to feel understood, loved, and accepted. My hope is that this book and these stories helped you feel validated in your own feelings, provided you with ideas and hope, as well as helped you learn ways to stay connected to your sibling and others in your life. Because what if, in the end, connection and love really are everything?

Photo Gallery

*Dani, Michael, and I in Colorado Springs
before he was deployed in 2003.*

During our visit with Michael on base at Fort Carson, where he was stationd.

Michael in one of his helicopters in Iraq.

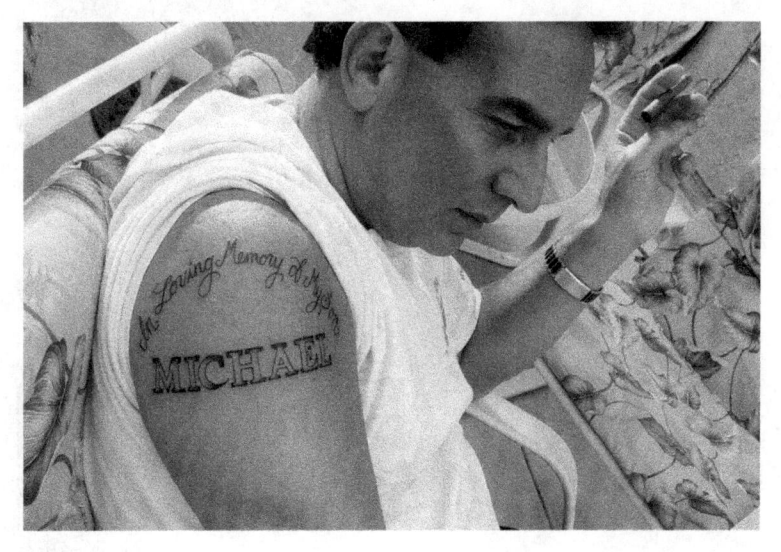

My father's first and only tattoo, in honor of Michael. 2004

The Army medical building in Fort Carson that was named after Michael, where he was previously stationed in Colorado Springs. This was an enormous honor. 2004

Mason picked #45 for his go-kart in honor of his Uncle Michael. January 2020, right before the Covid-19 pandemic put California, and much of the country and world, on lockdown for a while.

From left to right: My husband, Josh; my son, Mason; myself; my daughter, Mikayla; my mother, Carol; my father, Tony; my niece Ellie; my sister, Dani; my niece Natalie; and brother-in-law, John. In Avila, California, 2019. Photography by Ashley Christine.

Photo taken at Red Rock while we were visiting Michael at his base in Fort Carson, Colorado, before he was deployed to Iraq. March 2003. Our last family photo together.

CPSIA information can be obtained
at www.ICGtesting.com
Printed in the USA
LVHW082041041220
673103LV00005B/371